S.O.S.
The Story of the Life-boat Service

S.O.S.

The Story of the Life-boat Service

CYRIL JOLLY

CASSELL · LONDON

CASSELL & COMPANY LTD
an imprint of
Cassell & Collier Macmillan Publishers Ltd
35 Red Lion Square, London WC1R 4SG
and at Sydney, Auckland, Toronto, Johannesburg

and an affiliate of The Macmillan Company Inc, New York

First edition 1961
Second edition, revised and enlarged, with new illustrations, 1974

ISBN 0 304 29382 2

Printed in Great Britain by
The Camelot Press Ltd, Southampton
F 374

To my daughters
Elizabeth Pearl and Deborah Ann

Contents

Illustrations

Except where otherwise stated, reproductions are by courtesy of the Royal National Life-boat Institution

All the illustrations appear in Oliver Warner's *The Life-boat Service: A History of the Royal National Life-boat Institution*

Acknowledgements

I am grateful to the Royal National Life-boat Institution for permission to use information in the official *Journal* and in *Britain's Life-Boats* by Major A. H. Dawson, published by Hodder & Stoughton Ltd. I am also indebted to Mr. Patrick Howarth, Publicity Secretary of the Institution; Mr. Charles Vince for his invaluable advice and the use of material in his book, *Storm on the Waters*, and to the late Miss M. Caldwell of Dereham for reading the manuscript.

1 The Life-boat Service in Action

On 5th August 1941, when Britain had been at war for nearly two years, Convoy F.S. 559 was steaming slowly southward down the East Coast. Although it was August a gale was blowing and the seas were rough. It was night, and the ships were blacked out for fear of enemy submarines and aircraft. A sharp look out was also being kept for mines and E-boats. Danger in a dozen different forms had to be guarded against. So dark was the night and the weather so foul that the keenest eyes could see but little. There were no stars and no guiding lights, only heaving patches of foam showing lighter than the surrounding black waters.

The N.N.W. gale was driving the rain into the faces of the seamen so that it hurt like small shot. Spindrift from the waves mingled with the rain, but sailors and merchant seamen had to bear this discomfort and stare steadily into the night, for the seas were so rough that no man on watch dare relax his vigilance.

With the dawn the inky blackness gave place grudgingly to a cold mist. Visibility was almost as bad as in the darkness. The clammy vapour enveloped the slow-moving group of ships, and the seas grew ever angrier and more dangerous. Many an anxious discussion took place on the bridge of the ships, for the convoy was due east of Cromer, off the Norfolk coast, and on its port side were the dread undersea stretches of sand known as the Haisborough Sands where more ships have perished than on the famous Goodwins.

These sand-banks have been a nightmare to seamen for centuries. Innumerable ships have run on to them never to escape. The further a man sailed, and the more experienced he became in the ways of the sea, the more relieved he was when he got safely past these shoals in bad weather.

Neither the vigilance of the watch nor the skill of the helmsmen prevented the sands claiming their victims. Six ships, one behind the other, suddenly found themselves motionless although their propellers were churning the waters into a brown froth, and the engines raced madly. Bells rang imperiously as signals passed from the officers on watch to the engine-rooms calling for "Full speed astern". Six large ships, bringing cargoes invaluable to a nation at war, were firmly held by the sands. As men raced up gangways and along the decks, the sea-vapours swirled around them and the gale swept their urgent questions away over the waters. Around the ships the seas broke and seethed. The escort ships were flurried. Worried officers were asking what had happened? How had the ships got out of deep water into those dangerous shallows? That question is still asked. No one knows the answer. Possibly the flow of a strong tide aided by the gale pushed the ships further to port than they calculated. Navigation under such wartime conditions was a nightmare.

The news of the disaster flashed from the aerials of the two escort destroyers, *Wolsey* and *Vimiera,* to the nearest naval base, in code. For if sent in "clear" an alert enemy might intercept those appeals for aid and knowing that six ships were helpless on the sands, aircraft bearing the German black cross would soon try to make sure of their destruction. So strict were the security measures that the details received by the life-boat stations were scant—almost too scant.

Five life-boats, Sheringham, Lowestoft, Yarmouth and Gorleston and both Cromer boats, prepared to aid the helpless ships, although they did not yet know how many were in peril. The eight o'clock news was just being read.

Great hope was pinned on the Cromer boats, for the No. 1 boat, *H. F. Bailey*, could be launched in a matter of minutes into the roughest sea, from its slipway at the end of the pier, and the No. 2 boat should follow not long after. Moreover, the crews, led by their great coxswain Henry Blogg, had so often braved those sands they probably knew how to battle with their dangers better than any other men alive.

Henry Blogg told the crew of the *Harriot Dixon,* Cromer's No. 2 boat, to wait for the tide to fall before they attempted to launch from the beach. He could not give them much information other than to make for the southern end of the Middle Haisborough Sands.

The *H. F. Bailey* slid down her slipway at 30 m.p.h., hit the water and flung up the sea like an underwater explosion. Then she began fighting her way over the ocean to the scene of the disaster.

As the Cromer men neared the sands they heard the sound of distant aircraft and feared that German aeroplanes were hurrying to bomb the stranded ships. But it was an R.A.F. Hurricane patrol from a Norfolk airfield on its way to ward off any such attack.

When the *H. F. Bailey*'s crew saw six ships lying in their death throes together on the sands they gasped with awe and astonishment. Never had they seen or expected to see such a tragedy. The ships were the *Aberhill, Taara, Deerwood, Gallois, Oxshott* and *Paddy Hendly*.

At that very moment the *Harriot Dixon* was being pushed by a tractor into the heavy surf breaking on Cromer beach, and the Great Yarmouth and Gorleston boat, *Louise Stephens*, was also battling northwards to help.

The Navy had not been content to wait idly for the arrival

of the life-boats. About 8 a.m. as the *Taara,* with her back already broken, seemed in greatest peril, a small whaler from one of the destroyers braved the surf around the ship and rescued several of her crew. The work, however, was so dangerous and difficult that twelve merchant seamen were drowned in these attempts.

The *H. F. Bailey*'s crew saw that all the ships were in such peril there was not a moment to lose. The *Oxshott* demanded their first attention. The sea covered most of this vessel leaving only the upper deck, masts and funnel above water. But there was no sign of life. It looked as though all the crew had perished, so the life-boat turned and made for the *Gallois*. Then someone looked back quite by chance and saw with astonishment sixteen men roped to each other behind the *Oxshott*'s funnel. Their feelings as they saw the life-boat apparently abandon them can be imagined. Henry Blogg immediately turned back to save them. As he got close to the *Oxshott*, however, it seemed impossible that the life-boat could be manoeuvred anywhere near the desperate men. Great waves were sweeping right across the decks. Henry Blogg saw one thin chance of rescue—in the ship's upper works there was a crevice caused by the vessel breaking up. It was close to the funnel and the sixteen men. The coxswain saw that if he steamed over the submerged deck and thrust the bow of the *H. F. Bailey* into that opening and held it there it might give the seamen a chance to reach the life-boat. But if he made one miscalculation the seamen and his own crew would perish. It was a terrible risk; certainly not the sort of thing recommended in books of seamanship. Yet the situation was desperate and his crew were willing that he should try.

The coxswain swung the blue, white and red bows of his boat to point at the *Oxshott*. Then, with engines running "Slow ahead" he ran at the ship, as though to ram her. The *H. F. Bailey* rose on a wave over the sunken bulwarks, and thrust her nose into that jagged crevice.

The sixteen shipwrecked men had almost given up hope of rescue for soon it seemed the waves would reach and cover them. They saw the life-boat leave, then return. But how could it get to them? To their joyous amazement they realized the boat was coming straight at their ship, and in a minute the life-boat was actually on board with its oilskin-clad crew yelling to them to run for their lives. The stinging wind had reddened and roughened their faces. Salt glistened on hair and skin. They were stiff and sore but they somehow raised a cheer for their rescuers. In all their years at sea they had never seen such a feat of seamanship before nor would have believed it possible, but it had actually happened. They freed themselves from the rope that bound them to the funnel and dashed over the swilling upper deck a few at a time watching for the big seas that might so easily sweep them away. In their hearts they thanked God for the men who could not only do such an amazing thing with a boat but would do it for the rescue of strangers!

They could not all reach the *H. F. Bailey* before a powerful sea, rushing from the stern, forced her out of the crack. Again Coxswain Blogg put her back in the crevice and the remaining seamen were at last dragged over the guard chains into the life-boat.

The seas had already punished the *H. F. Bailey* by banging her on the deck of the *Oxshott*, and at any moment a wave might smash her to pieces like an egg dropped upon the dairy floor. It was time to get away. With the *Oxshott*'s crew safely aboard, the *H. F. Bailey*'s engines were speedily reversed and she backed away from her position on the doomed ship.

The *Gallois* was still above water. Thirty-one bedraggled men clung to her rails hoping and praying for rescue. They had been there for hours watching and feeling their ship go to pieces under them. It could not last much longer. Time was all important for them and for the life-boatmen. To moor the *H. F. Bailey* alongside would take many vital minutes, so, keeping the boat's head to the seas, Henry Blogg decided to use his engines and helm to stay beside the wreck. The engines were kept running just fast enough to counter the force of the seas. It needed great seamanship and flawless co-operation between coxswain and mechanics, but it was done and all the seamen slithered safely down ropes or leapt on to the heaving decks of the life-boat.

The *H. F. Bailey* was now crowded; her crew were so hampered they could not work properly. The forty-seven rescued men were taken to one of the destroyers riding in deep water, and while they were being transferred the *Harriot Dixon* arrived. Jack Davies, Cromer's second coxswain, was put aboard from the *H. F. Bailey* as he already knew how the seas were running on the sands. He headed for the *Taara,* and quickly saved eight men who still remained on that wreck.

The *H. F. Bailey* went now to the *Deerwood* where nineteen men were crowded together on the highest part of the bridge waiting anxiously for help. Their ship was practically under water when the Cromer boat drew near. Again Coxswain Blogg threw normal tactics aside, for time was the over-riding factor, and once more he drove the damaged life-boat over submerged decks.

As he brought the boat up against the bridge he watched each approaching sea, for to be caught unawares in such a position meant disaster. There was no convenient crevice here but there was sufficient water to allow him to use his engines to hold the life-boat in position while the nineteen men clambered aboard. Every member of the *H. F. Bailey*'s crew was tense and excited for they all knew their position was so precarious that a false move would be fatal.

At last it was done; the wrecked men were safe aboard and the propellors threshed in reverse, pulling the life-boat off the *Deerwood*'s deck. Another hazardous rescue had been achieved by brilliant seamanship.

The next ship was the *Aberhill,* lying in a welter of surf. But the *Louise Stephens* was already there, tied up on the lee-side, rescuing the survivors. It had taken her three hours against the gale to reach the sands. Now her coxswain, Charles Johnson, was shouting to the twenty-three remaining men to jump into his boat. When the men were all saved another cheer went up from the watching destroyers where keen eyes were marking through binoculars every move in this great drama of the sea.

The last ship to be helped was the *Paddy Hendly*. Her end was very near, yet twenty-two men were still on her disintegrating decks. Henry Blogg spun the helm and set the *H. F. Bailey* towards her. He juggled with the currents and pieces of wreckage to get alongside. Again he kept his station by the wreck giving "quick-fire" instructions to his mechanics and using only his engines while over a score of seamen leapt into his boat as it rose on the crest of each wave.

And now it was all over; the *H. F. Bailey*'s work was done; she turned to leave those terrible sands, and every man heaved a deep sigh of relief as she fought her way out of this pounding surf. Then in a twinkling the swift hand of calamity tried to claim them and turn their triumph into defeat. While they worked, the tide had been steadily dropping and the *H. F. Bailey* was laden with fifty-one men. The life-boat was low in the water and suddenly it bumped once, heavily. Then again. There were startled cries. Henry Blogg gripped the wheel and looked anxiously around. The wheel was unresponsive—his boat was helpless on the sands. Nothing he or his crew could do would save them. The greatest of all life-boatmen was as powerless as a child to prevent disaster. A huge wave bore down upon them on the port side. As it towered above their boat, its curling crest became white with foam, every man clutched some part of the life-boat and thought the end had come. But instead of crashing down upon them in a hammer-blow of tons of water the towering billow miraculously lifted the boat and swept her forward towards deep water. It was a great deliverance.

The *H. F. Bailey* put the rescued men aboard a destroyer and limped into Yarmouth for repairs.

Three holes had been knocked in her hull and twenty feet of fendering had been torn from her sides. The stem had been wrenched off and some of its bolts forced right into the air cases behind.

The *Louise Stephens* had already landed twenty-three rescued men, the *Harriot Dixon* eight, and the *H. F. Bailey* had saved eighty-eight. The Sheringham and Lowestoft boats had also fought their way round the coast, but when they reached the sands the six merchant ships showed no sign of life and the sea, cheated of its prey, was continuing its work of destruction.

When the Convoy F.S. 559 resumed its voyage six total wrecks were left behind on the Haisborough Sands and thousands of pounds' worth of cargo and equipment was being tossed about by the waves.

The R.N.L.I. gave Henry Blogg its highest award, the gold medal (the V.C. of the Life-boat Service). He also received the British Empire Medal. Jack Davies and Charles Johnson both received the Institution's silver medal and many of the crew got the bronze medal. Never were medals better earned.

2 How It All Began

The splendid service to Convoy 559 is typical of the readiness of life-boatmen to risk their lives for strangers imperilled by shipwreck. And long before there were any life-boats men would put out even in little fishing cobles to aid those in danger. But there is another side to the story, for not so long ago in our history some men were so inhuman they deliberately caused wrecks. These wreckers hung out false lights to lure ships on to the rocks so that they might plunder the cargo and profit from the ruin of others. The mariner was faced not only with the perils of the sea, but with this sort of treachery on the shore. The lights that he thought were guiding him into the harbour led to destruction.

In the eighteenth and nineteenth centuries swarms of small craft sailed around our coasts. In the year 1800, fifty thousand sail are reported to have passed the port of Great Yarmouth. From Newcastle large numbers of small ships brought coal by sea to London and the south, for there were no railways. These vessels were often unseaworthy and wrecks were common. A storm with the wind blowing on the shore was certain to cause a number of disasters. People on the beach had to stand helpless and see the sailors drown because there was nothing they could do to save them. There was no boat that could face such a storm.

Among the folk distressed by these wrecks was the Archdeacon of Northumberland, Dr. John Sharp. He had seen or been told of vessels wrecked at the mouth of the Tyne where large numbers of coal ships converged. The Archdeacon was in charge of a sum of money to be used for charitable works, one of which was for aiding seamen. He determined to use some of it to get a boat made which would be able to go out to wrecks through the broken water of the shore. He learned that a coachbuilder, named Lionel Lukin, who came from Dunmow in Essex but was living in London, had been experimenting with a Norwegian yawl trying to make it safe in rough waters. Lukin had put three watertight compartments and a cork gunwale in his boat for greater buoyancy, and a heavy false keel to keep it upright and give it stability. Lukin proudly termed his boat *Unimmergible*. He patented his ideas.

Lukin let a pilot of Ramsgate use this boat to test its qualities, and he never saw either the man or the boat again. It was known to have crossed the Channel when other boats dared not put out and it is strongly suspected the *Unimmergible* did excellent service on smuggling duties!

He built a second boat called the *Witch,* then, in 1786, the Archdeacon sent Lukin a coble to convert into a boat which could be specially used for saving seamen from wrecks. When this had been done it was placed at Bamburgh in Northumberland. So Lukin's third effort became the very first life-boat, and Bamburgh the first life-boat station in England and, as far as is known, in the world.

The centuries of passive acceptance of the toll of lives and property by shipwreck was changing to a determination to try to reduce that grievous loss. This resolve was strengthened when three years later a terrible shipwreck occurred at the mouth of the Tyne. A ship named *Adventure* ran ashore and began breaking up close to the beach where thousands of watchers had gathered. So furious was the surf nobody could help the wrecked seamen and one by one they dropped off into the sea. Feeling was strong among the onlookers and a meeting was at once called at South Shields by members of a social club known as Gentlemen of the Lawe House. They offered a prize of two guineas for the best model of a boat which could be used to reach wrecks.

When the news got about, a man named William Wouldhave, a teacher of singing and a house painter, decided to submit a model. He was an inventive man and had long been thinking about making a life-boat. One day when chatting with a woman at a well he had toyed with a wooden dipper floating in her pail. Suddenly he stopped playing with the utensil; he had noticed that no matter how he pushed the dipper under the water, as soon as it came to the surface it righted itself. In fact, it was self-righting and that was just the quality he wanted in a boat. With a feeling of excitment Wouldhave went away to see if he could include this principle in a life-boat. He made and tested a model. To his great joy it worked so he submitted it to the club. The judges, however, awarded him only half the prize. Wouldhave was understandably annoyed, for he was poor and badly needed the money. It is believed he told the judges just what he thought of such niggardliness and strode away in anger refusing to accept the guinea. But he left his model. Later, when he had calmed down, he said that if he had not received the prize, at least he had the satisfaction of knowing that his idea would be used to save life.

The Gentlemen of the Lawe House asked a boatbuilder named Henry Greathead to build a boat on the lines of Wouldhave's model, but with some alterations including a curved keel and without the power to self-right. This Greathead did and it was called the *Original*, for it was not a conversion but was the first boat to be specially built as a life-boat. The cost was £150. The *Original* was 30 ft. long, carried twelve oars and had seven hundredweight of cork for buoyancy. The boat was narrow and rose sharply at bow and stern. She was kept free of water by baling. For forty years after her launching in 1789 she went out to wrecks and saved hundreds of lives at the mouth of the River Tyne, until she was finally smashed on the rocks.

Several years passed without another boat being built. Then the Duke of Northumberland, who had been greatly interested in the *Original*, gave Greathead an order to make a boat. The Duke was so pleased with it that having placed it at North Shields he presented another to the Portuguese who were our allies against Napoleon.

Lloyd's, the great corporation of underwriters, formed a committee and subscribed £2,000 to establish fourteen life-boats at various places. This scheme kept Greathead busy for some time. By 1803 he had built thirty-one boats.

It is good to know that Lionel Lukin had not finished with life-boats. The Suffolk Humane Society asked him to supervise the building of a 40 ft. sailing life-boat at Lowestoft to reach the dangerous sands off the Norfolk and Suffolk coast. It was launched in 1807 and was used for over forty years saving more than three hundred lives. It was the first of that fine type of boat, long used on the East Coast, known as the "Norfolk and Suffolk".

During these early years the development of life-boats was undertaken by individuals or local societies and that was how things remained until Sir William Hillary, the founder of the Life-boat Service, took up the cause in 1823.

Sir William was born in 1771 of a Yorkshire family. As a young man he had sailed a small boat round Malta and Sicily. The experience gained during those trips came in very useful later.

In the dark days of 1803, England lived under the threat of invasion by Napoleon. Measures were taken to fight him if he landed and Hillary showed great ability and energy in raising a force of 1,400 Essex men for home defence. This was the largest number recruited by any individual and Sir William spent £20,000 equipping them. For this patriotic work he was made a baronet. But he was so reduced financially by these expenses and the failure of some plantations in which he had invested money that in 1808 he had to go and live in the Isle of Man where taxation was lower. He settled at Fort Anne in the Bay of Douglas.

Humanity was, however, to benefit by Hillary's adversity, for when from his home above the bay he saw many ships thrown ashore by the fierce storms that raged around that coast, the sight of men drowning only a stone's throw from the land roused him to action and provided a new cause to champion. In the year 1822, twelve vessels were blown into Douglas Bay and wrecked. Hillary saw most of those disasters, but unlike other people present he could not just stand and watch. He was determined to help. He procured a boat, and although it was not suited for such hazardous work, went to the aid of the distressed men. In that year he led several rescue attempts and saved eighty-four lives. In addition, he was moved to write his historic "Appeal to the British Nation", which led to the foundation of the Life-boat Institution.

The Appeal shows the kind of man he was. It aimed at the heart and the head. It pointed out the terrific material loss to the nation because of shipwreck; the widespread misery caused through the death of so many men, and the effect on the morale of all seamen. To tackle such a great problem, Hillary said, needed more than the generosity and energy of a few fine people or local societies: it must be a national concern supported by all men of goodwill. In Sir William Hillary's own words: "It is a cause which extends from the palace to the cottage, in which politics and party cannot have any share, and which addresses itself with equal force to all the best feelings of every class in the State." There should be no favouritism as to who should be saved first; foreign seamen ought to be treated as our own. Nationality, colour or creed should not be considered—the test was to be need! (In some years one-third of the men saved by British life-boats are from foreign ships.) The men who manned the boats must be recompensed for their labours, and if they lost their lives in the attempt at rescue their dependants should be helped and not left to fend for themselves.

Hillary's Appeal gained wide sympathy and support, but it might never have become more than an appeal had it not been for Thomas Wilson, M.P., a London merchant. He was so struck by the noble aim and the practical details of Hillary's plan that he made the cause his immediate concern and called a meeting at the City of London Tavern on 12th February 1824. A number of interested people attended that first informal meeting and agreed that a national organization should be formed to preserve life from shipwreck; to relieve the needs of those rescued; to recompense the men undertaking the work; and also care for the families of those who lost their lives in such endeavours.

A general meeting was held three weeks later. In that brief interval the sponsors of the scheme worked extremely hard. They obtained King George IV's consent to become Patron; and secured five royal dukes and Prince Leopold as Vice-Patrons, the Prime Minister as President, and a large number of important people as Vice-Presidents, among them the Archbishops of Canterbury and York.

Without dissent twenty resolutions were passed at that historic meeting on 4th March 1824, and the National Institution for the Preservation of Life from Shipwreck came into being. It was the first in the world although the Dutch people followed suit only a few months later.

The management of the Institution was to consist of a patron, president, governors, a committee of forty, a treasurer, three trustees, three auditors and a secretary.

Among those present at that meeting were William Wilberforce, the fighter against slavery, and Captain George Manby, inventor of the life-saving rocket.

The successful launching of such a great enterprise was a source of joy to Sir William Hillary and a year later the Institution awarded him a gold medallion in token of his magnificent work in founding the Institution.

At last there was an organization to deal with life-saving at sea on a national scale. Throughout the country there were many local associations owning life-boats, and doing fine work in saving life, but gradually these societies have been taken over by the Institution. They included:

Anglesey Association
Dorset Shipwreck Association
Dover Humane Society
Lincolnshire Coast Shipwreck Association
Norfolk Shipwreck Association
North Devon Association
Suffolk Humane Society
Sunderland Local Life-Boat Society
Tees Bay Life-Boat Society

While his great Appeal was being launched Hillary set to work to form a district life-boat association in the Isle of Man. Douglas already had a station and by his own efforts he got three other stations established in six years. To estimate such an achievement it should be remembered that there were then only forty-five stations around the whole coast of the United Kingdom.

Again Hillary did more than establish stations and make his moving Appeal, he went out in the life-boats. He was a leading member of the Douglas crew which had had one of Greathead's life-boats in 1802. Again and again he set an example of courage and skill that inspired his men.

In the year 1825 he led a splendid mission to the *City of Glasgow* and saved sixty-two lives; he also rescued nine people from a sloop, and eleven from a brig. Five years later, when he was sixty-three years old, Hillary received the Institution's gold medal for his finest deed—the service to the Royal Mail boat *St. George.*

The *St. George* was blown into Douglas Bay in a fierce gale. The life-boat was new and not ready to be launched. It seemed that no help could come from the shore, but Hillary would not stand by idle. He persuaded his crew to take out the boat, and after a tremendous struggle they reached the wreck. Twenty-two men were taken off, but it was almost the end of Hillary's career for he and three others were washed overboard by a tremendous sea. He was so battered by the water that his chest was crushed and six ribs broken. But he stuck at his post until the rescue was completed.

Such injuries at his age should have made the Institution's founder give up this arduous work. It took him a long time to recover, but the next year he was again at the helm, and when he was sixty-five he saved fifty-four men from the wrecked *Parkfield.* Altogether Hillary led various crews in saving 305 lives, and he won three gold medals.

Right up to his death in 1847 he continued to help those suffering from shipwreck. At the age of seventy-six Hillary tried to establish in the Irish Sea a Harbour of Refuge for stormracked vessels—a place where they could find shelter from the tempest. Here again this was no hare-brained scheme, but one so practical that seventy years later his proposals formed the basis for improvements to Douglas harbour.

He secured the erection of a Tower of Refuge in 1832 on a rock off Douglas where seamen wrecked in Douglas Bay could find safety until the storm abated. He also worked hard to establish a School of Navigation with the aim of improving seamanship and thereby avoiding unnecessary shipwreck.

After a life devoted to the service of his country and his fellow men Hillary was overtaken by sorrow and misfortune. The loss of his wife was followed by financial ruin; he had to leave his fine house, and died soon after, in January 1847.

People flocked from all over the island to pay their tribute to his generosity and life-long labours for humanity. But the funeral was at night, and no name was put on the tomb because it was thought that the body of a bankrupt man could be seized to pay his debts. It was a pathetic end to a noble life.

Just how much the life-boat service in the Isle of Man owed to Hillary's endeavours is shown by the fact that five years after his death the stations he had so painfully established fell into neglect and remained so for many years.

In 1921 Hillary's tomb, which had become disgracefully dilapidated, was renovated by the Institution and the following inscription placed upon it:

> "He founded in the year 1824 the Royal National Life-boat Institution, and in 1832 built the Tower of Refuge in Douglas Bay. Fearless himself in the work of rescue from shipwreck, he helped to save 305 lives, and was three times awarded the Gold Medal of the Institution for great gallantry.
>
> 'What his wisdom planned, and power enforced,
> More potent still his great example showed.'
>
> Thomson."

The founding of the Institution had been most encouraging and the response from the nation was splendid. But often new societies start well and then interest gradually fades. It was so with the Life-Boat Institution. The first year nearly £10,000 was subscribed and arrangements were made to establish fifteen life-boat stations; five years later, however, the annual income had dropped to just over £300. That sum was pitifully inadequate to maintain existing life-boats in proper order. The decline was due to many causes other than the fickleness of the British public. Those early years were beset with grave difficulties for the whole nation; riots were common, and financial chaos, in which many banks closed, prevailed throughout the country. With ruin and unrest on every hand it was not to be wondered at that a new venture should lack assistance. Moreover, the R.N.L.I. had yet to learn how it could best enlist the financial help of its well-wishers.

It is to the credit of those in charge that although the Institution's income melted like an ice-cream in the sun, they still tried to carry out their obligations, including the encouragement of individual acts of life-saving, and they awarded over two hundred medals in the first twelve years.

One of the most glorious of such deeds was performed in 1838; no finer act of heroism is on record and the central figure was not a powerfully built life-boatman—it was a twenty-two-year-old girl whose health was beginning to fail, Grace Horsley Darling.

Grace was born in November 1815, the year of the Battle of Waterloo, at Bamburgh in Northumberland where the first life-boat had been placed. Her father, William Darling, was the keeper of Longstone lighthouse in the Farne Islands.

On the night of 6th–7th September 1838 a gale sprang up and sent waves crashing around the lighthouse, making sleep almost impossible. Between 4 a.m. and 5 a.m. both the lighthouse-keeper and his daughter were peering out into the storm. It was keen-eyed Grace who first saw through the mists of spray and spume a vessel on the rocks of a nearby island. The vessel was the 400-ton pleasure steamer *Forfarshire,* bound from Hull to Dundee, with sixty-three people on board. Seven of the crew of the *Forfarshire* had got safely away in a small boat before the ship was lifted on to the rocks and broken in two. The afterpart was then swept away with most of the passengers. All perished. The survivors on the forepart had reached a small rock and lay there for hours numbed with cold and swept by the seas in a gale so fierce that most of their clothes were torn off them.

William Darling had only a coble, but Grace urged him to try to reach the vessel. The lighthouse-keeper hesitated, not for fear, but because of the awful risk that he must take. He knew that it would be a bitter struggle for himself and his daughter to row a boat to the wreck even with the tide helping. They could certainly not get back unless they were successful in landing on the rocks and rescuing some of the shipwrecked men and getting them to help with the rowing. The price of failure must be the death of himself and his daughter. Grace also realized the danger yet she was willing to go.

William Darling made his decision and so began a rescue that has stirred the world to admiration for over 130 years. Together they launched the open rowing boat 21 ft. long and 6 ft. wide. Pulling for nearly a mile through seas that threatened their destruction every moment, they reached the rocks. Then, with incredible skill and coolness, Grace managed the boat single-handed while her father landed on the rocks.

William and Grace Darling got four men (one injured) and a woman, who had lost both her children, into their boat then pulled back to the lighthouse. While Grace looked after the injured, William Darling, with two of the rescued men to help him, returned to the wreck and took off the last four survivors. The heroic lighthouse-keeper and his daughter had saved nine lives.

The Humane Society awarded them each a gold medal and the Institution a silver medal for their great courage. When the public at last learned of this heroic deed a subscription was organized and Grace was made a national heroine.

Grace Darling's health was giving way and the strain of that terrible night hastened her illness; she lived only four years after this epic rescue, dying of consumption on 20th October 1842. She was buried in Bamburgh church, and the boat is preserved in a special building near by. Her name and example have been and will be, while lives are endangered at sea, an inspiration to men and women of all races.

In the years following, various designs of life-boat were put into service; the Liverpool Dock Trustees in 1840 built nine boats known as the Liverpool type. Mr. Pellew Plenty, Mr.

George Palmer, Messrs. Lamb and White of Cowes all introduced different designs incorporating considerable improvements.

The economic conditions of the country were so bad during the "Hungry Forties" that rightly or wrongly the committee of management of the Institution felt it was useless to make any appeal for funds. The outlook for the organization was gloomy in the extreme; many of the boats were unfit for duty and the whole fabric of administration was crumbling. A great expansion of the work was badly needed but it was out of the question, there was not enough money even to keep going! So things drifted and declined until 1849. The Institution had then been in existence for twenty-five years and the public as a whole had forgotten or been allowed to lose interest in the venture despite the fact that 6,716 lives had been saved in that time.

The thing that roused the country to its responsibilities was not another eloquent appeal or an epic rescue, it was a disaster! Again the mouth of the Tyne was the stormy setting. On 4th December 1849 a ship ran aground and the South Shields life-boat went to her aid. The boat reached the wreck—*Betsy*—and got alongside. She was just going to take off the crew when a heavy sea rebounded from the wreck and flung most of the life-boatmen overboard. The following wave capsized the boat. She remained upside down and was swept ashore. Of her crew of twenty-four, twenty perished. The four that were saved would also have been drowned but for the gallantry of two other life-boat crews that had seen the disaster and immediately went out to their aid.

A disaster on such a scale to men who had given outstanding service for their fellows stirred the nation. It called attention in a dramatic way to the work of the life-boats as no words could do. The committee of management seized the opportunity to tell the British people of the neglected state of the service. Gear was obsolete, woodwork was rotting, half the ninety-six boats in the fleet were unseaworthy; everything was deteriorating through one fault—lack of public support. Economic

AN APPEAL

TO THE

BRITISH NATION,

ON THE

HUMANITY AND POLICY

OF FORMING

A National Institution,

FOR THE PRESERVATION OF

LIVES AND PROPERTY FROM SHIPWRECK.

BY SIR WILLIAM HILLARY, BART.

LONDON:
PRINTED FOR G. AND W. B. WHITTAKER,
AVE-MARIA-LANE.

1823.

Title-page of Sir William Hillary's
'Appeal to the British Nation . . .' 1823

Medal of the Royal National Life-boat Institution.

Obverse: portrait of Sir William Hillary as Founder, by A. G. Wyon. Reverse: Scene of rescue, by William Wyon, R.A.

'Sir William Hillary and Manx Life-boat going to the help of the steamer *St George* in Douglas Bay, 1830.' Painting probably by Samuel Walters of Liverpool

Grace Darling (1815–42), by William Joy (1803–67)

Lord Prudhoe, later Duke of Northumberland, President of the R.N.L.I., 1851–65. Miniature of 1844 by Sir William Charles Ross, RA, hitherto unpublished

'Life-boat and Manby Rocket Apparatus Going to a Stranded Vessel Making a Signal of Distress, 1827.' By J. M. W. Turner, R.A.

Model of Beeching's prize design life-boat, 1851. She was 36 feet in length, with an iron keel and raised air cases fore and aft. She pulled 12 oars and was rigged with a lug foresail and mizen

Life-boat of 1872 built by Forrestt of Limehouse for the United States Revenue Marine Service. Length 30 feet, pulled by 12 oars, and built of double diagonally planked mahogany. The cost was about £250

Vice-Admiral J. Ross Ward,
Chief Inspector of
Life-boats, 1852–83

Richard Lewis,
Secretary, R.N.L.I., 1850–83

Sir George Shee,
Secretary, R.N.L.I., 1910–31

Charles Dibdin, Secretary,
R.N.L.I., 1883–1910,
in Court dress

conditions had improved considerably and men who had not previously given money or helped the life-boats in any way dipped into their pockets and also took an active interest in the work. So, from that sore loss of life on the Tyne sprang a new public enthusiasm. Again the seeds of sacrifice, sown on those troubled waters, brought a harvest of blessing. Helpers such as the Institution had long needed but never found came forward, and from that dread day the work never looked back.

The first thing the committee did after the Tyne disaster was to invite Algernon, Duke of Northumberland, to become President and reorganize the service. The office of president had been vacant for twenty-three years. They could not have done better, for the "Sailor Duke", as he was known, had the experience and the qualities that were needed for the task of reorganization. He brought enthusiasm and a spirit of dedication to the work of rebuilding the tottering Institution. Queen Victoria had been Patron since her accession in 1837, and the Duke set out to enlist new helpers. The Prince Consort became a Vice-Patron and many gifted and generous people, fired with the Duke's zeal, came on to the committee of management.

The Duke of Northumberland aimed at an immediate improvement in life-boat design. In 1851, the year of the Great Exhibition, he called for models, offering a hundred guineas as a prize, and another hundred to build a boat from the winning model. Great interest was aroused and 280 entries were received, many of which were curious—some were crazy! There were folding boats, boats made from rushes, gutta-percha, and even a canvas covering over wickerwork. It would have been difficult to find a crew to take such a boat out in a North Sea gale! The prize was won by James Beeching of Great Yarmouth. His 36ft. boat was clinker built (the planks overlapped), and weighed two tons. She carried twelve oars, which were essential to get clear of the surf or to approach a wreck, and had a lug foresail and mizen. Beeching's boat was the first genuine self-righter, for her high end cases filled with air and the heavy keel, as well as two tons of water ballast, brought her up the right way after a capsize. She was placed at Ramsgate and did splendid work, finally dying of old age.

This boat was a complete success, and was the beginning of what, with a few alterations, has until recent years been the self-righting boat of the Institution. She has played a tremendous part in the history of the service.

In that same contest a model of a steam life-boat was submitted but it was not taken up, for there were grave difficulties about using steam. In 1890, however, the first steam life-boat was built and placed at Harwich. It was called the *Duke of Northumberland.* Only six steam boats were used by the R.N.L.I.

In 1854 the title of the Institution was changed from "Royal National Institution for the Preservation of Life from Shipwreck" to the "Royal National Life-boat Institution". The work of helping people saved from wrecks was taken over by the Ship-wrecked Fishermen and Mariners' Benevolent Society. That society in turn handed to the R.N.L.I. some life-boats which it had established. So, in happy partnership, the two organizations continued the work.

This was the end of the beginning.

3 After Reorganization

The zeal and ability of the Duke of Northumberland which had started the work of reorganization of the Institution marked the beginning of a new epoch in its history. The new spirit which he fostered soon animated the service and was apparent not only to workers and life-boatmen closely connected with the cause, but to the whole country. People who had never been interested in life-boats now gave money regularly and freely. Legacies and gifts came in from all quarters, and for the first time they were used directly to build new life-boats. The donor chose a name for the boat. In some cases organizations such as friendly societies, universities or the Civil Service, named a boat. Various towns also set themselves the task of paying for a life-boat and giving it a name. The first to do so was Ipswich. That is how we have had such life-boats as the *Mary Stanford*, the *City of Edinburgh*, and the *Civil Service.*

Once the public was alive to the needs of the Institution, support was most encouraging, and the more people came to know of the work the more they supported it. In 1865, fourteen years after he had begun the task of reorganization, the Duke of Northumberland died. The thriving life-boat Institution was a magnificent monument to his labours.

In the same year, thirty-four new life-boats were added to the fleet, bringing the total to 144; nineteen were added the next year, twelve the next, and so the growth continued. Representatives from other countries started coming to Britain to study our service, and to place orders for life-boats.

Britain has a long coast-line for its small area and much of it is busy with passing ships—busier than any in the world. The men who started and ran the life-boat service knew they could not prevent wrecks from happening; so they aimed at putting life-boats at the most perilous places along the five thousand-mile coast-line so that when a ship did get into difficulties every effort would be made to save those in danger.

The year 1870 was one of terrific gales; every village and town around Britain had a story to tell of great storms, wrecks and heroic rescues. The Institution's fleet, which had grown to 220 boats, did wonderful work and saved 1,231 lives. Not one life-boatman lost his life. It was one of the best years the Institution ever had.

There were many magnificent rescues in that stormy year but the most renowned of all pulling and sailing services was the mission to the *Indian Chief* which took place on 5th January 1881.

The *Indian Chief* of 1,238 tons was on her way from Middlesbrough to Yokohama, manned by a crew of twenty-nine. She was sailing through the night off the Kentish coast. At 2.30 a.m. her pilot sighted the Knock lightship and was trying to steer the vessel through a network of shoals, but a very strong, bitterly cold wind was making his job most difficult. Then things began to go wrong. Knowing his ship was drifting towards the Long Sand the captain tried to put her about, but the main braces fouled and she missed stays and continued to drift. By frantic efforts the crew got her on to another tack, but it was too late, the spanker boom sheet fouled the wheel and the ship was blown broadside on to the Long Sand. The vessel struck the Sand with a force that threatened to smash her to pieces.

The sails flapped and cracked against the spars and masts like giant whips. The masts themselves bucked and jumped under the strain. Fear seized the crew. Feverishly they sent up rockets and lit flares, then watched the sea and sky for answering signals from the lightships.

Soon after, the clouds scurried from the heavens and the stars appeared. It cheered the men and brought new hope. Then rockets rushed up into the star-studded darkness seeming to tell them their plight was known and help would soon be coming. But had they known just how tardy that help would be and what suffering they must endure, they would probably have given up in despair. Many a man who watched the rocket showers sprinkle the darkness never lived to see the Ramsgate life-boat ride into the furious surf around them in one of the greatest of all sea rescues.

Impatiently they waited for help, drenched and half-frozen. The minutes ticked away in such intense discomfort that only a man who has suffered shipwreck can imagine it. Every hour sapped their strength and lowered their hopes. But at last the darkness was driven off by a cheerless dawn as the day broke over the waste of waters.

It was hardly daylight when one of the crew cried out above the wind's uproar that he could see a life-boat sail. The whole crew rushed along the tilting decks and, regardless of the spray that drove into their faces and stung like whipcord, they watched the boat trying to get nearer. It could not, however, face the huge waves breaking around the wreck. Again and again the unknown vessel attempted to get near but at last she dipped into a trough of the seas as though to hide her face because she could not help, and disappeared. That sail had spelt hope; when it had gone, the wrecked seamen turned away from the rails with despairing groans.

It was not a life-boat that had attempted to help the *Indian Chief* but a fishing smack, and although the fishermen had tried magnificently to aid the crew, they realized that to venture into the surf breaking on the sands would be suicide. The gallant little smack therefore turned away to battle to the land and seek help for the wrecked vessel.

With heavy hearts the men of the *Indian Chief* took shelter in the deckhouses and cabins. Their ship was lying well over on her side and the rising tide bumped and banged her viciously until she broke completely in two. Terror then laid hands, colder than the icy wind, upon the men. They thought their last moments had come. A wild attempt was made to get the boats launched. Three were actually let down but one was snatched from the ship and overwhelmed immediately. The two men in it were lost. Their comrades were sobered and knew this was not a way of escape but of certain death. They struggled back to the wave-swept cabins, and lived a lifetime of anxiety, as the hours of misery dragged by.

What suffering they would have been spared had wireless been in use, for no news of the disaster reached the shore until 11 a.m.—nearly nine hours after the *Indian Chief* struck the sands! A fishing smack, probably the one that had attempted a rescue, struggled into Harwich with tidings of the wreck.

On the *Indian Chief* noon came and slowly passed. The afternoon dragged by. Then, at 5 p.m., a monstrous sea rose and swept the broken ship from end to end. By a miracle no one was carried away, but without a moment's delay the crew scrambled from the cabins into the rigging, away from the waves. Seventeen men got into the mizen-mast and ten into the foremast. They lashed themselves there with ropes. Those who were already too numb to tie the ropes were secured by their shipmates.

When the daylight went the cold grew even worse. Every sea that rolled hissing over the ship took more of her timbers. From the leaning masts the red-eyed, exhausted men looked down, watching their ship being slowly gutted, until only the frame-work of ribs and masts still stood. The sea around was littered with flotsam.

Suddenly the mainmast cracked like a cannon and crashed downwards. In doing so it struck the mizen-mast where sixteen men were lashed and brought it down in a tangle of destruction. The lashed men stood no chance of escape and their cries were silenced by the sea.

Half an hour later the survivors, almost dead with cold and grief, saw a light appearing and disappearing on the water. It gave new hope and when dawn came at last the dim shape of a steamer was seen in the distance and soon after a more thrilling sight—a life-boat sailing towards them! Their joy cannot be described. They wept like children, the tears running down their salt-caked cheeks, red and raw from the lashing of that bitter wind.

That life-boat, with sail spread like a sea bird, was the 42 ft. *Bradford* of Ramsgate. Forty-two-year-old Coxswain Charles Fish, with piercing eyes scanning the wreck and dark beard soaked with spray, stood at the helm. He had been coxswain already for nine years, and in the twenty-one years he was in charge of the Ramsgate boat he helped to save no fewer than 877 lives. Few boats have had such a busy time as the *Bradford.* Charles Fish became known as one of the best coxswains of the service, but in stories of his fine missions his name was always linked with the *Indian Chief.*

When the news that a ship was on the sands reached Ramsgate, orders were given to get the paddle tug *Vulcan* away to tow the life-boat to the sands.

The wind, which had swung to the N.E., had such an edge that one life-boatman likened it to a flaying machine, and Coxswain Fish said it made his face feel "as if it was being gnawed by a dog".

The seas tossed the *Vulcan* like a cork, lifting her so high that the coxswain said, "You could see her starboard paddle revolving in the air high enough out for a coach to pass under." At times the tug was almost smothered by the waves; only the stern could be seen. Yet she wallowed and staggered into the seas, slowing down so often that the life-boatmen repeatedly thought she was giving up the fight. The master of the tug, however, had the same spirit as the life-boatmen. He knew if he turned back the life-boat would never get to the sands, so he kept his bows towards the Knock because fellow-men were in great danger.

Every man in the life-boat was drenched in spite of his oilskins as soon as they were half a mile at sea. They tried to fix up a sail as a shelter from the wind but it only lasted two minutes before it was whipped away in ribbons.

At 4.30 p.m., when darkness was descending, the Kentish Knock lightship was seen, and half an hour later the life-boat got near enough to hail her and find out where the wreck was lying. Then the tug steamed on while both crews looked for the ship, peering ceaselessly into the deepening darkness until their eyes burned from the lashing of wind and spray. At last they knew it was useless to go on; the only thing possible was to lie up all night. That would mean hours of intense discomfort and the danger that they too might be overwhelmed by the seas.

Every member of the crew realized the risk, yet they all urged Charles Fish to take it. The tug was, therefore, signalled and the master of the *Vulcan* agreed to this course. Throughout the night he kept his paddles turning just fast enough to keep the tug from dropping astern.

In the life-boat two men kept watch while the rest tried to make a shelter and get some protection from the wind. Again they rigged up a sail and thirteen of them crept under it to lie there in a heap of arms and legs, seaboots, oilskins and life-jackets. Even with this windbreak they were so numb from cold that the hard knocks received as they rolled about were not even felt. Coxswain Fish was a teetotaller, and he did something that night most unusual for him: twice he passed round the rum bottle because the cold was causing his men so much suffering.

Hour by hour crept past with the stout tow-rope keeping

the tug and boat together as they battled to stay head on to the waves. When the dawn appeared a keen-eyed young man on watch suddenly yelled, "There she is! There she is!"

The men scrambled stiffly out of the shelter and peered in the direction of his pointing finger. The air was full of driven spray, but as the *Bradford* rose on a wave they saw, three miles away, a slim mast, only a mast, rising from the heaving white waters. This was the wreck they had come for—but it looked as if they were too late! They hurried to their stations, slipped the tow-rope, hoisted the storm foresail and, leaving the tug, drove before the wind towards that mast. As they rapidly neared the wreck they saw the strife of waters around it, and could see and hear above the roar of the wind and seas hitting their own boat the waves rising in great columns round the *Indian Chief* and crashing down on her with the noise of thunder. The strong tail wind lifted the salt water thirty feet high and flung it in solid sheets right over them, to crash down sometimes twenty yards ahead of their fast-running life-boat.

No one, however, was heeding the cascades of flying spray. The men clung grimly to the boat but kept their eyes on that pencil-like mast, for there was a strange blob on it, something like a sail, but not a sail and not part of the mast—it must be men. As they got closer they could distinguish seamen and shouted gladly that the whole ship's crew was there—they little knew that sixteen men were still lashed to the mast that had fallen into the sea four hours earlier!

Fifteen fathoms from the *Indian Chief* the *Bradford* anchored and dropped down on her cable to the wreck. The eleven men clinging to the mast unlashed themselves and climbed or were helped down the rigging. One of them threw a line and float which the Ramsgate men secured. The *Bradford* was hauled under the lee of the wreck and one by one the numb, half-dead men were pulled into the life-boat.

The *Bradford* hauled on her anchor away from the wreck and after a grim fight reached the waiting tug and was towed back to Ramsgate. A great crowd had gathered to welcome the rescued men. The story of their suffering and salvation was told by Clark Russell, the writer of sea stories and reporter of the *Daily Telegraph*, and all England echoed with the praise of the men of Ramsgate.

The R.N.L.I. honoured their God-fearing, lionhearted coxswain, Charles Fish, with its highest award—the gold medal.

It seems a pity to turn from such an exciting rescue to the dull subject of money, and yet the two are closely linked. To be able to station life-boats where they are needed and keep them in a state of efficiency depends on how much money is coming in for such a purpose.

Although the Institution's income was rising during the "eighties" the rapid growth of the work outstripped it—often by tens of thousands of pounds. Once again it was a disaster that taught the grim lesson that to maintain such a great service without state grants needed far more money than was being received—in that year, 1886, the Institution received £33,000 less than it required.

The disaster happened off Formby in Lancashire on 9th December 1886.

It was a German barque, the *Mexico*, which had become stranded in a gale on a shoal between Southport and Formby. The tide was running against the wind, and the sea was looking for prey. The crew of the *Mexico* was saved by the Lytham life-boat. Two other life-boats, from Southport and St. Anne's, also went out but were capsized and two men only were saved. Twenty-seven lives were lost on one service. It was the greatest of all life-boat disasters, but it did much to inspire the public to start the Saturday Fund enabling badly needed money to be raised for life-boat work. That fund was the forerunner of the present life-boat flag day.

There was a man on the spot at the time who was able to bring home to the whole nation just what such a calamity meant to a little fishing village—there were fifty orphans and sixteen widows to mourn the loss of the men—and to point out that if these men could give their lives for their fellow men the public could surely give adequate financial support. His name was Sir Charles Macara, a great figure in the industrial and social life of Lancashire. On his doctor's orders he was resting at St. Anne's from the hectic life of industry, but he often accompanied the fishing boats to sea, and became much concerned with the life-boat's activities. After the disaster he immediately started a fund to help the dependants of the dead men and the splendid sum of £33,000 was given by people from all over the country.

With that task completed Sir Charles Macara began studying the administration of the Institution. He found that two-thirds of the money raised for life-boats came from little more than a hundred people, and saw that far more funds were needed if the great work was to continue. In 1891 he launched an appeal through the Press to bring the Institution's income up to £100,000 a year.

Throughout the north the newspapers took up the plea. Someone suggested a Life-Boat Saturday, and the idea caught on. Many towns in Lancashire and Yorkshire made it a gala day with bands, processions, concerts and carnivals. Manchester and Salford alone raised £5,500 in their effort, and in twelve months the contributions from the great linen and wool counties increased from £3,000 to £21,000.

The scheme appealed to towns in Scotland and south of the Humber until the idea of Life-Boat Saturday had spread over Britain. It was purely a voluntary movement of well-wishers and was neither started nor controlled by the Institution. A Ladies Auxiliary Committee was also formed to collect regularly from subscribers in their homes and so help the Saturday Fund. This committee did splendid work for many years until taken over by the Institution in 1910. Then eleven years later, when the Ladies' Life-Boat Guild was formed by the Institution, the voluntary women workers found full scope for their organizing ability and enthusiasm.

The large increase in revenue resulting from the Saturday Fund allowed the service to expand and this went on until 1909 when the Institution was spending nearly £100,000 a year and it was evident that the work must either be curtailed or income stepped up to keep pace with expansion. Hitherto the Saturday Fund efforts were entirely unco-ordinated and it became obvious that if the fund was administered by one authority it would be far more efficient and less money would have to be spent in raising money. So in 1910 the Institution took over all the work of raising its own funds and thanks to the tact and skill of the new secretary, Mr. George Shee, the period of transition was passed without loss of goodwill or revenue. In fact, contributions increased right from the beginning and so far as is known the Institution never lost a helper.

4 The Development of the Modern Life-boat

The development of the modern life-boat is a fascinating story. The era began in 1887 when Mr. George L. Watson designed the first Watson boat. It was a pulling and sailing boat but non-self-righting.

The St. Anne's disaster had shaken faith in the self-righting principle, which had been hitherto considered by all but a few stations on the East Coast to be the solution to the problem of life-boat design. In fact, in the thirty-five years following 1831 whenever new stations were established, in almost every case they had been equipped with self-righters. Now it seemed that greater stability to prevent capsize was better than the power to self-right after an upset, so the Institution set up a permanent technical sub-committee to improve design and Mr. Watson, a famous yacht designer, became consulting naval architect. Bringing his wide experience to bear on the problem he decided to plan a new type of boat. He put the emphasis on stability and set aside the principle of self-righting because it impaired steadiness in high winds. The new boat was bigger, faster and more seaworthy.

In 1903 he saw the possibilities of the internal combustion engine in life-boats and encouraged by the committee of management and aided by Captain E. du Boulay, R.N., the pioneer work began. To the great credit of the committee of management they did not wait until the fitting of engines was thrust upon them, but began their inquiries right at the beginning. It was a tremendous development and was eventually to change the entire aspect of life-boat work, for it brought what every coxswain needed—power; power to push on against wind and tide; power to range further out to sea; power to manoeuvre; and power to stay away from the station for long periods if fuel and provisions could be taken out. Summing up—that added power meant far greater effectiveness in life-saving.

When the experiments began the motor car was still a novelty and the petrol engine anything but reliable. An unreliable engine in a life-boat was a greater risk than in a car. There were other problems to be overcome, for a life-boat has to work in far worse conditions than any car. The engine must run in fair weather and foul without attention, and at all sorts of angles as the boat pitches and rolls. The controls have to be simple so that they can be operated by touch in the dark. The engine demands air, but no contact with salt water which would soon corrode and ruin it. In addition, for a self-righting boat, the engine must cut out automatically if the boat capsizes so that when she rights herself she does not sail gaily away and leave her crew floundering in the water.

The first experiments began at Cowes with the fitting of a 9 h.p. Fay & Bowen engine in the *J. McConnell Hussy*, a pulling and sailing boat. When the conversion was finished in 1904, this boat was placed at Tynemouth. There, Captain H. E. Burton of the Royal Engineers was Honorary Superintendent, and intensely interested in petrol engines. He took up the tests with enthusiasm, but the local fishermen did not think much of the smelly, noisy engine and would not form a crew for the converted boat. The captain, however, got soldiers from his unit to man the boat for eight months, by which time the fishermen had seen what it could do and had changed their views.

There were so many technical problems that as soon as one thing was put right it seemed another went wrong, but Captain Thomas Holmes, R.N., the Institution's Chief Inspector, tackled them all. Not until 1910, however, when a boat fitted with a Blake engine covered fifty miles a day for eleven days without serious mechanical trouble, was the real promise of the motor life-boat shown—the promise that was fulfilled in 1915 by the *Henry Vernon,* at the *Rohilla* rescue.

For over half a century the experiments with motor power have gone on, and the Institution has used every modern invention which would increase the efficiency of its fleet.

Right up to 1923 no life-boat was entirely dependent upon an engine; sails were always provided as they were for purely sailing boats. But the motor life-boat had become so trustworthy that in that year the first boat was built relying absolutely upon its engines. It had to be a twin-screw in case one engine failed. The brilliant designer of this boat was Mr. J. R. Barnett, who had taken over Mr. G. L. Watson's task. The Barnett twin-screw could carry 150 people and at that time was the most powerful and best-equipped life-boat in the world. The length was 60 ft. and there were two 80 h.p. petrol engines. She had two cabins, in one of which hot food and drink could be prepared. A net was fitted amidships so that when the boat came alongside a wrecked seaman might jump into it and avoid injuries often incurred when leaping on to a hard deck. This boat was too large for a slipway or carriage, and could only be stationed where there was a safe anchorage.

While life-boats relied upon sails, even as auxiliary to engines, the cockpit had to be kept aft so that the coxswain could watch his canvas. With the change to all-motor power it was possible to bring the helmsmen's position nearly amidships and this allowed much better handling of the boat.

The first diesel engines were fitted to the Yarmouth, Isle of

Wight, boat in 1932, and today every new life-boat has a diesel engine, for with diesel fuel the risk of fire is reduced and the boat can travel further on the same quantity of spirit. The engines are cooled by a closed water system. The fresh water circulating around the engine flows through tubes in containers in the bottom of the boat and the cold sea water constantly passing over them makes a most efficient system.

It would be a great economy to the Institution if one type of boat would suit all stations, particularly in building boats and holding spares. But that is impossible, for conditions vary greatly from place to place. At one station a heavy boat can rush down a slipway into deep water; at another, the boat must be taken over a wide flat beach to be launched and the lighter it is the better. At some stations work lies close to the shore in shallow waters, at others the boat has to go far out to sea and must be able to stay out for a long time. So there must be several different types of motor life-boats.

PRESENT-DAY TYPES OF LIFE-BOAT

Today we are experiencing a revolution in life-boat design. Novel and exciting things are happening. The Institution, which has sometimes been criticized for being bound by tradition, is forging ahead with many projects. The yardstick of crew safety remains, but over twenty boats are now being built or are on order.

In 1958 the re-equipment of the fleet began with self-righting boats of the 37 ft. Oakley class, which takes on water ballast at launching, and if capsized rights herself in a few seconds by transferring the ballast from one tank to another. As a life-boat afloat has an expected life of twenty-five years, or thirty if housed (with a further ten years in reserve), re-equipping is a long as well as costly business.

A Mark II version of the Oakley dispenses with water ballast and she rights herself by virtue of her profile. A larger Oakley boat of similar design, 48 ft. 6 in., is also in service. There is also the Solent type of the same dimensions having a steel hull.

Two 70 ft. boats, like small trawlers, went into service in 1965. One, stationed at Kirkwall in Orkney, has done magnificent work.

To meet the demand for faster life-boats the Institution has built six "patrol" type boats based on a U.S. Coast Guard design, but with steel instead of aluminium hulls, 44 ft. long. They have a top speed of 20 knots and an endurance range of twenty-six hours. The *Khami*, stationed at Gorleston since 1967, has delighted her crew and done great work. Rescues have been effected with but three crew members.

The *Arun*, built of cold-moulded ply, 52 ft. long and a draught of but 4 ft. 9 in., has a hull designed for twenty-eight knots, but so far her top speed has been under 20 knots.

The introduction of small inflatable Inshore Rescue craft, in 1962 was revolutionary, and these boats today are saving more lives than the conventional boats. Development in type of hull and floorboards is constant since their introduction. The most modern *Atlantic 21*, has a rigid bottom and a speed of 28 knots. Over 113 Inshore boats were operating last summer.

Some stations still have the Liverpool 35 ft. 6. in. self-righter, and the larger 42 ft. Watson cabin boat with its big sister of 47 ft. Several stations continue to use the 52 ft. Barnett boat of twenty-nine tons.

CONSTRUCTION

Most of the Institution's life-boats are built in the Isle of Wight. Construction depends very largely upon wood and the world is scoured for the most suitable kinds. The hull is made from African mahogany, with a layer of calico and white lead between the double skin of planking. English oak, unequalled for strength, is used for the stem and stern-post of the boat. Gunwales and timbers are also of English oak. The decks are of mahogany; the keel of Burmese teak; and Western red cedar is used for the air cases which are packed into every available part of the boat to make her so buoyant that if a dozen holes were knocked in the hull she still would not sink. These air cases, which are covered with calico and painted, sometimes number nearly three hundred. In addition, the boat is divided by bulk-heads into watertight compartments.

Copper and naval brass are evident everywhere. Aluminium alloy is now largely used for canopies, cabins and bulkheads, and for the scuppers along the sides of the hull. These simple valves hinged on the outside allow the weight of water on the inside of the boat to open the flaps, and the water gushes out. Outside the boat, however, their weight or the pressure of the sea shuts them. So effective are these scuppers that they can clear the water from decks and cabins almost as quickly as the sea can throw it in. Steel is now being used for hulls in some new models, and G.R.P. (glass reinforced plastic) is used for the McLachlan-type boats.

GEAR

No boat is better equipped than a life-boat and the gear it must carry seems large, perhaps too large, until one remembers that lives may be lost through not having the right equipment at the right place.

The *drogue*, or sea-anchor, is the oddest yet most interesting item of gear, and it is so important that an official of the R.N.L.I says, "I would rather be without wireless than the drogue in bad weather." It is a conical canvas bag, rather like a wind-sock, which is thrown out astern when a boat is running before a heavy sea. It has a tripping line attached to the small end and a thick rope to the large end, and when the small end is to the fore the bag offers little resistance to the water, but when a big sea is bearing down upon the life-boat the tripping line is slacked bringing the large mouth of the drogue to the front. The water, rushing into the big opening, must force its way out through the small end. Thus the drogue acts as a brake, has an invaluable steadying effect, and keeps the stern of the boat down giving greater rudder control. As soon as the danger is passed the other end of the line is slacked so that the drogue is tripped and resumes its former position. This simple apparatus helps to prevent the boat broaching, and has probably saved more life-boatmen's lives than any other piece of equipment.

An interesting modern aid for the coxswain is the *Kent clear view screen*—this is a revolving glass disc fitted to the windscreen to throw off spray and rain. It serves the same purpose as the windscreen wiper of a motor car.

A *searchlight* is carried, enabling rescue work to go on during the darkest night. At one time it was worked by dissolved acetylene but is now electrical.

Signalling lamps, and a *deck floodlight* are fitted to the aluminium alloy *mast* which is usually collapsible so that the boat can enter under the lintel of its boathouse doors. The exhaust pipe from the engines is incorporated in this mast.

The *line-throwing gun* is an important item by which communication is often established between a life-boat and the vessel in trouble. When the projectile is fired it carries a line over the ship, enabling a stouter line for the breeches buoy to be hauled aboard. Up to the year 1922 the heaving line had to be thrown by hand, usually by the bowman. For all his skill the distance he could throw was very short, but the gun has a range of over eighty yards. There are no firing sights, the angle for holding the gun is automatically indicated. A line-throwing pistol is now replacing the gun.

A *loud-hailer*, which is mounted on deck, can be heard distinctly at four hundred yards. It is worked through the boat's radio set and saves the coxswain's lungs, enabling him to talk to shipwrecked men, the crew of a light-vessel or helpers on the shore.

The *anchor* is the most important piece of gear. It is often used in rescue tactics to get alongside a wreck as well as for its normal purpose of holding the boat. The standard type is called the "Fisherman"; a few fathoms of chain attach it to a 90 ft. nylon or wire cable.

Oil. Amazing rescues have been made possible by "pouring oil on troubled waters". This oil is carried in special tanks and is sprayed not poured on the sea.

Life-belts. The original cork life-belts gave place to ones with kapok filling, but in 1967 the R.N.L.I. introduced a new life-jacket and protective suit which does not impede the wearer when working. It automatically brings a man thrown overboard face upwards in the water. Made of neoprene proofed nylon, impervious to water and oil, it has a light, a whistle and a life-line.

Radio telephony was introduced into Rosslare Harbour life-boat in 1929. Since then improvements have been many and constant. By 1970 the standard medium of communication between shipping and the shore was VHF, so today all life-boats have it and can talk to ships in distress, to the shore or to helicopters. It has supplanted ultra high frequency for this purpose. Reliable range is over 100 miles and the Cromarty life-boat was heard in the Scilly Isles, 550 miles away, on one occasion! The mechanic usually operates the set. An echo sounder for determining the depth of water under the boat is also part of the electronic equipment.

The Institution encourages all life-boatmen to learn first aid and insists that at least two members of each crew should be proficient. This is not a question of red tape. It is a matter of life and death. Often the early application of correct first aid treatment can save a life, and artificial respiration, if promptly applied rather than delayed until the patient is landed, can tip the scales in favour of survival. So a large *first aid kit* is carried.

Survival suits are not in the kit but are a modern aid to restore body temperatures of those suffering from severe exposure. The patient is placed in this suit of rubberized fabric which is inflated and the temperature of the body is soon increased.

A naval-type *stretcher* to hoist an injured person aboard,

axes, paraffin stove, flares, ropes and *lines,* all with a special purpose, are needed as well as *binoculars, charts, parallel rulers* and *dividers* for navigation. *Provisions* include blankets, cocoa, chocolate biscuits, corned beef and self-heating soup.

LAUNCHING

Great strides have been made in recent years in launching life-boats. Concrete or steel slipways enable the boat to plunge into deep water and get on its way in a few minutes. Horses, which once played a noble part in this work, have been superseded. The last time horses were used was at Wells in Norfolk in 1934. Today a crawler tractor can do the job that formerly needed half a dozen horses and forty or more men. Launchers often suffered injuries when battered by heavy surf or from exposure; the tractor has cut that peril out wherever it is used.

The Institution uses three main types of launching tractor: Case/Roadless LA; Fowler Challenger Mk3, and Case 1000D. They sometimes have to work in the sea up to a depth of seven feet and will haul a boat on its carriage (fourteen ton load), up a 1 in 4 gradient. Being watertight, if they get stuck in the mud and have to be left, even if the sea covers them no harm will be done. Powerful brakes will hold both boat and carriage in very steep places. The controls, such as gear and clutch levers, are extended so that the driver can operate the tractor even if his cockpit is under water.

Launching a boat by tractor is relatively simple; the tractor takes the carriage to the sea, it is then unhooked and going to the rear pushes the carriage into about three feet of water. Two ropes fastened to hooks on the boat's keel pass to pulleys on the front of the carriage, and then come back under the carriage. These are connected to the tractor so that when it reverses rapidly, moving away from the sea, the ropes are tightened and the boat is shot from its carriage into the water, where its own engines take over.

The most remarkable launch on record took place during

the night of 12th January 1899, on the north coast of Devon.

At 7 p.m. the Lynmouth coxswain received a telegraph message from Porlock saying a large ship was in trouble in the bay. But the Lynmouth boat could not get away because the seas, pushed up by a westerly gale, were breaking across the harbour mouth. They must abandon the ship to its fate or take their boat thirteen miles overland to Porlock and launch from there. That meant climbing to 1,400 feet from sea level, cutting down banks, demolishing walls and knocking down gateposts, with only feeble oil lamps to show the way and a furious gale blowing.

No further message came from Porlock for the wires were blown down, but Coxswain John Crocombe and his second, G. S. Richards, decided they must try to help the ship and would make the attempt to get to Porlock. The honorary secretary, Rev. A. R. Hockley, sanctioned this. Most of the crowd thought such a task utterly impossible and said so, but every man and woman in the village, not to mention twenty horses, turned out to get the life-boat up the famous Countisbury Hill—with a gradient of 1 in 4½.

A small party with a horse and cart went ahead bearing shovels and pickaxes to dig down banks at narrow places and make sufficient width for the carriage to pass.

At 8 p.m. the main party started. They soon knew what a struggle lay ahead. The horses would not pull together and were difficult to manage. The oil lanthorns were continually blown out by the wind. Half-way up the hill a wheel came off the carriage, caused by repeated knocks against the rocky banks. After a long delay the carriage was jacked up and the wheel refitted with another linch-pin. Reaching the top of the hill the launchers pressed on over this exposed part of Exmoor, a thousand feet up. The wind and rain made every yard a battle and many drenched, exhausted helpers turned back. But twenty struggled on.

They caught up the advance party which had dug down banks

and a wall, but found the carriage would not go through a mile-long lane, in many places only seven feet wide. Still undaunted they took the boat off the carriage and used the quietest horses to pull it along the lane. The men placed skids six feet apart and took turns to carry them to the front as the boat passed over them. The carriage was sent over the open moors. Somehow they got through the narrow lane, and found the carriage waiting. The boat was put back on wheels and the party carried on over Hawkcombe Head, 1,400 feet above the sea, to the top of Porlock Hill.

Then they were faced with getting the heavy load, the heaviest then known, down the hill.

"How can we possibly get round these dangerous corners with such a string of horses and the carriage?" was the question most men asked. But the drivers believed it was possible, so with all the men hanging on drag ropes and using safety chains they started down the gradient. All went well until at the bottom of the hill some cottages made the road too narrow for the carriage. The launchers were not to be stopped; a wall was pulled down. As they were doing it an indignant old lady emerged scolding the men for waking her, pulling down her wall, and bringing "that thing" down the hill. She had never seen a life-boat! When told what was happening, however, she stopped scolding and went along with the boat.

A party from Porlock met the Lynmouth men and told them they could not reach the beach by the low road as the sea had washed parts of it away and broken down the sea wall. So they took the high road. It meant cutting down a small tree that impeded their path, but the beach was reached at 6 a.m.—ten hours after they had started.

Without taking food the crew launched the boat and reached the ship at 7.30 a.m. Some of the life-boatmen went on board and helped to get the *Forest Hall* and her crew of fifteen to safety.

So ended the epic launch of the Lynmouth life-boat.

5 The Men and Women who make up the Service

What sort of people make up our life-boat service? The answer is—all sorts! From the Queen of England who gives her gracious support as Patron to the fisher-boy who eagerly hauls on a rope to launch a boat. It is truly a *National* institution. People of all ranks, creeds and politics man, maintain and launch the boats, collect the money, and carry on the administration. The crews are all volunteers. They are not conscripted. If they do not want to get out of bed in the middle of the night to go out on the stormy sea, no one can make them. There is no compulsion—except the compelling urge to help those in peril.

Until recent years the life-boats were manned almost entirely by longshore fishermen—men who fish close to or along the shore—but in the last thirty years the number of such fishermen has dwindled rapidly. Many fishing villages have now lost all their fishing boats and men. Even large fishing towns have to rely on people whose jobs lie ashore to man the life-boats when need arises. For example the Great Yarmouth and Gorleston life-boats are now manned by three fishermen, a shipwright, a storekeeper, a shopkeeper, a carpenter, a labourer, and the coxswain is a drifter owner. In just a few places life-boats have relied mainly on men who were not fishermen, as at

Newbiggin where many of the crew are coalminers; Cresswell in Northumberland, before the station was closed, was also manned chiefly by miners in the Ashington pits, and at Donna Nook (also closed) in Lincolnshire the crew were all or mostly farm workers.

The life-boats, however, are still chiefly operated by fishermen, for crews are smaller; six or eight men man a motor life-boat whereas thirteen or more were needed to work the pulling and sailing boats. Moreover, fewer boats are needed; two motor life-boats will do the work of at least five pulling boats. So the fleet which once numbered 308 now consists of 135 station life-boats and 116 inshore life-boats. The last pulling boat went out of service in 1957.

When the maroons crack over the sea calling the crew together the fishermen leave their tasks; mending nets, painting boats or landing a catch, and run for the boathouse. If their relatives know that they will need their seaboots or coats they also hurry with them to the boat. There must be no delay, for a minute saved can mean a life saved! Modern life-boats have actually been battling the waves within four minutes of the maroons sounding; so the crew did not have time to comb their hair, or shine their boots!

Sometimes the men are fishing when the call comes. It happened so on the East Coast when the fishing fleet was at anchor attending to crab-pots near the shore. The signal was heard, and the boats, lying comparatively still, suddenly stirred to great activity. Anchors were hauled, lines dropped and many boats hurried to the beach, some with engines running, others under sail. Then, while friends held the boats, the men scrambled ashore, and made for the boathouse. It is an unwritten law that a man puts the service first. He leaves whatever he is doing to get the life-boat launched. That sometimes means a big sacrifice, but it is done.

Of course, the crews are rewarded by the Institution for their work. A fixed scale is paid according to the time of day and year. The coxswain receives a retaining fee and the mechanic is paid a regular wage to keep the boat ready for instant use. This system of reward is only fair, for most of the crews are working men, and sometimes they are away from their jobs for a day or more. Their families would suffer seriously if they were not recompensed for their services. But that does not make them employees of the Institution. They remain volunteers. This principle was laid down by Sir William Hillary, the founder of the R.N.L.I. No monetary reward, however, compares with the risks and hardships the life-boatmen endure. The power that drives them on is not money but mercy.

Until tractors were used or slipways built to launch the boats, horses, men and often women had to haul the boat into the water. Sometimes there were as many as sixty launchers, pulling at long ropes, pushing at shafts and wheels to get the heavy boat over a rough beach into the sea. At most stations there were plenty of men to do such a hard job, but in some villages women had to share this task or the boat would never have got away. These brave women have turned out at all hours of the day and night, and in the worst of weather to launch the life-boat, often with their own menfolk on board. Sometimes it meant wading waist deep in icy water for hours as the sixty launchers of Holy Island in Northumberland did in wind and stinging snow in 1922. Twenty-five of that gallant team were women.

Boulmer, in the same county, was also noted for its women launchers—headed by Mrs. Stephenson, wife of the coxswain—and Cresswell too was such a village. In 1874 it had no life-boat; a sudden summer gale caught a fisherman and his three sons when they were well out at sea in their coble. One of those who watched the men's vain struggles and saw them drown was the fisherman's daughter, Margaret Brown. For forty-eight years after that, when Cresswell had a life-boat, she took her place with other women launchers and never missed a service or a practice.

In January 1876 the Cresswell life-boat received her first call to a wrecked steamer. To reach the best spot for launching, men, women and horses dragged the boat half a mile along the beach in the teeth of the gale and launched her. Meanwhile one of the steamer's boats, with four men in it, had broken away from the wreck and capsized. The men clung to its keel. The women of Cresswell then clasped their hands and formed a living chain with Margaret, at the far end, completely out of her depth. Four times she reached the upturned boat, and, clutching a seaman, helped him ashore.

The life-boat had been unable to reach the wreck and returned. It was then decided to send for a life-saving rocket apparatus which was kept five miles along the coast. No man could be spared to take the message but Margaret Brown volunteered, and with two other fisher-girls set off to run along the lonely coast track. They reached a river and found the swollen waters had carried away the plank bridge. At the risk of her life Margaret made two attempts to cross the river and finally succeeded. She then helped her companions over. The track led over the moors, but the gale was so fierce the exhausted girls could not face it. They climbed down to the beach where it was more sheltered. The three struggled along between sea and cliffs with their feet torn and clothes ripped to ribbons, until they reached Newbiggin. There Margaret's two companions were so dead-beat they had to be left at a cottage while she stumbled on. She reached the coastguard station and collapsed, unable even to give the message she had suffered to bring. But the coastguard knew her and guessed her errand. The apparatus was taken by horses to Cresswell—only to find the life-boat had at last managed to reach the wreck and had saved three women and seven men. The brave girl later became Mrs. Margaret Armstrong, known in the service as the "Second Grace Darling"!

Another heroic woman of this station, Mrs. William Brown, known as "Kitty", in the year 1876 saw three fishermen in a coble unable to make the harbour in a rising sea because of the size of their boat. Although she tried she could not recruit any help, so, single-handed, she launched a small boat and rowed through the waves. Although exhausted, she reached the fishing coble and the three men were able to use her boat to get safely to the shore.

The magnificent self-sacrifice of these launchers ranks with the finest deeds of life-boat crews.

It needs more than boat crews and launchers to keep Britain's life-boats afloat—it needs money, £3,500,000 a year. And women have proved the most ardent and successful collectors. One woman has raised over two thousand pounds and the fishwives of Cullercoats in Northumberland, near Whitley Bay, have made a name for themselves in this work. Dressed in their coloured shawls they have organized special collections year after year, and one old but most persuasive lady at times filled five collecting boxes and raised over thirty pounds in a few days—that was when a pound was a lot of money!

Life-boat work often runs through whole families, and round our coast some families have become famous for their devotion and courage in the service.

Since 1824—the year the Institution was founded—the Cables of Aldeburgh have served in life-boats for five generations. Two of the family have given their lives in the work; Thomas Cable, the first Aldeburgh coxswain, was drowned when the life-boat capsized in 1859 while crossing a shoal to reach a stranded ship. His son had already sacrificed his life; he swam to a wreck with a line enabling seven men to be rescued, but he himself was drowned when the line broke. The most famous of the family was James Cable who died in May 1930, aged seventy-eight. He was coxswain for thirty years, and triple winner of the Institution's silver medal; he held the Humane Society's silver medal, and received its thanks on vellum three times for saving drowning persons from the shore.

On the coast of Lancashire, at Formby, north of Liverpool, the family of Aindows has provided the greater part of the life-boat crew for sixty years. At one time there were thirteen Aindows in the crew.

In 1862 the Formby life-boat went out in a terrific gale, and all but three of the crew were drowned. One of the survivors, Henry Aindow, was found next day almost dead under the upturned boat which had been washed ashore. That would have made many men avoid life-boats for ever, but not Henry. When the new crew was formed he became coxswain with six sons and two grandsons serving under him. Such is the spirit that pervades the service.

The Robsons live at North Sunderland, in the far north of England. A life-boat has been there since 1827—and a Robson in the crew. In 1838, when Grace Darling helped her father to row to the *Forfarshire,* three Robsons, who were members of the local life-boat crew, got news of the wreck at Seahouses and put out with four other men in their own fishing boat. After a bitter fight they reached the ship to find only dead seamen on board; Grace and her father had taken off the living. Their position was so hazardous that they took refuge at the Longstone lighthouse after skilfully negotiating a gap only twenty yards wide where the tide ran like a mill race.

It was in 1908 that Coxswain James Robson took his boat to the rescue of the Norwegian ship *Geir,* wrecked on the deadly Knavestone Rock. They could not get near the wreck but the coxswain went overboard with a line, swam to a rock and connected another line from the steamer. A stout rope was thus passed from the ship and fourteen men went down it to the life-boat. James Robson was then hauled back to his own boat.

The Browns of Cresswell (the men made up the crew of the life-boat, their wives, daughters and younger sons were the launchers); the Stantons and Stephensons of Boulmer; the Davies, Allens and Balls of Cromer, are but a small fraction of the fine fishing families whose names are linked with the life-boat service.

The spirit of high endeavour seen in the crews and launchers runs through the whole service; it is shown by its honorary workers such as branch secretaries and collectors. Branch secretaries, receiving no pay, are a vital part of the movement. The service could not operate without them for they are to a great extent liable for the efficiency of the boats and crews. Theirs is the responsibility of deciding whether the life-boat should go out. Of course they consult the coxswain, but it still requires considerable knowledge of local conditions and seamanship to make such a decision. Many have insisted on going out with the life-boat and sharing the dangers and hardships of the crew. On one service a pulling and sailing life-boat had just crossed the harbour bar in a gale when a sea broke over the boat. It knocked every man down, swept away all oars and carried the boat right back into the harbour. But the crew rallied, and using spare oars and the sail went on to reach a wrecked schooner. They took off eight men just before the vessel's three masts crashed down. It was the branch secretary, present in the boat, who took the helm when crossing the harbour bar to relieve his coxswain, and like him received the silver medal for gallantry and later the coveted gold badge.

Women with collecting boxes, secretaries and honorary superintendents dealing with correspondence and technical problems form part of the host who give the best of their talents and and energies to keep the life-boats ready for any emergency. Many of them never set foot in a life-boat yet they play an essential part in the work of life-saving.

6 Great Coxswains

The coxswains of the R.N.L.I. are a picked band—the finest of a magnificent brotherhood. They are the spearhead of the army of life-boatmen, and on them falls the heaviest burden of responsibility. Their courage must inspire the life-boat crews to face the storm's sharpest dangers and their judgment and skill must outmatch its violence. To wear a coxswain's life-belt is a mark of honour. It means the wearer has been chosen for his leadership and devotion to a great cause; chosen by the very men who will put their lives in his hands. The best traditions of the service are symbolized in him. But the greatest coxswains are the first to pay tribute to the qualities of the men who make up their crews.

In the 150 years of the Institution's existence there have been many hundreds of coxswains—at one time there were 308 life-boats—and a high tribute could be paid to each one, but from that gallant company only a few can be mentioned here.

Robert Smith of Tynemouth
1849–1927

Coxswain Robert Smith of Tynemouth will always be remembered and honoured as one of the finest coxswains of the service. For fifty years he was associated with the Tynemouth life-boats, being coxswain from 1910 until he retired in 1920 at the age of seventy-one. Along the north-east coast, famed for its brave deeds of life-saving, his name became a household word. His courage and skill stirred men's hearts.

Born at Cullercoats in 1849, Robert Smith became second coxswain of the Tynemouth boat in 1909. The next year he became coxswain. He was a pioneer of motor life-boats. The first boat converted to motor power (a rowing boat fitted with an engine) was placed at Tynemouth. In 1911, as coxswain of that station, he commanded the *Henry Vernon*, one of the earliest motor life-boats. It was with this boat that he battled over forty miles in pitch darkness and in full gale, to aid the hospital ship *Rohilla*. It was one of the greatest exploits of the life-boats. For that service he received the gold medal.

In January 1913 the Tynemouth motor boat received a call to assist the S.S. *Dunelm* which had grounded near Blyth east pier in a S.E. gale, and the crew had been forced into the rigging. The Blyth pulling and sailing boat could not get off and the Tynemouth boat was sent for—but it was ten miles away. Such a furious sea was breaking in the mouth of the Tyne that some of the usual crew held back, feeling conditions were too bad to launch their boat. Many people in the crowd that had gathered also urged that the *Henry Vernon* should not put out. Coxswain Robert Smith, however, felt that they could weather the great seas and, therefore, ought to go. Although he could not get a full crew, which increased the danger, he still decided to set out. Captain H. Burton, the superintendent, took charge of the engine in the absence of the mechanic. They launched the boat with a crew of only five. This was a tremendous test not only of the quality of the motor life-boat but of the Tynemouth crew.

Those who had urged against the launching were even more alarmed and amazed that their boat should put out with such a small crew. But Robert Smith gripped the wheel and made his

Depot at Poplar, East London, nineteenth century, showing life-boat transporters used on open beaches, once pulled by horses and later by tractors, to get the life-boats into positions from which they could be launched

Depot at Boreham Wood, Hertfordshire

Hydraulically propelled steam life-boat *Queen* on trials in 1897 on the Thames, with Rennie's Waterloo Bridge in the background. Built by Thornycroft, 55 feet in length, the *Queen* had an active life of twenty-six years and was the means of rescuing 196 people

Lord Mottistone and the crew of the Brooke, Isle of Wight, life-boat preparing for a routine exercise

Famous coxswains;
Charles Fish of Ramsgate, leader of the *Indian Chief* rescue of 1881

James Cable of Aldeburgh, wearing old-pattern life-belt with knife-holder

Robert Smith of Tynemouth, conspicuous in the *Rohilla* rescue of 1914

Robert Cross of the Humber, outstanding in the Second World War

Steam paddle-tug towing life-boat to wreck, nineteenth century.
Painting by G. N. Nibbs (1816–93), hitherto unpublished

Famous coxswains:
John McLean of Peterhead,
gold medal, 1942

Patrick Sliney of Ballycotton,
gold medal winner for the Daunt
Rock light-ship rescue of 1936

Richard Evans of Moelfre, twice
awarded the gold medal of the R.N.L.I.

Herbert Petit of Guernsey,
awarded a gold medal in 1963

il and motor: the Sheringham life-boat, 1936

Mrs Margaret Armstrong, of Cresswell, Northumberland, 1849–1928, who for fifty years never missed a launch of the life-boat

boat meet the towering seas head on. With his deep-set eyes screwed up against the wind, his naval-type beard wet with salt spray, he looked the embodiment of determination and courage. He believed it was his duty to go, and nothing would turn him back.

The *Dunelm* was reached after an hour's terrific battle. Somehow the *Henry Vernon* got alongside and took off all the crew from their perilous holds in the rigging. Then the Tynemouth men turned to come back, and with the wind and seas behind them it needed all the seamanship they knew to control their boat. One sea did, in fact, catch the boat with such force it flung Coxswain Smith to the deck, knocking him almost unconscious. He was therefore unable to steer the boat, and another member of the crew took the helm. But they got back safely with the men that had been saved from certain death. The risk had been worth while. For this mission Coxswain Smith received the silver medal.

A local paper describing that rescue said it was "one of the most daring and remarkable achievements in the history of the Tyne life-boat station." That was no exaggeration.

It was the same Robert Smith who went three times to the Norwegian steamer *Beesheim* in November 1916, when it was thrown on to rocks in the River Tyne. The life-boat made its way among the dangerous boulders, and by splendid seamanship rescued the entire 111 persons.

Having chalked that fine "score" on the rescue record board the motor life-boat went out the next morning to a steamer which had grounded in Blyth Bay. The wreck was submerged when the *Henry Vernon* reached it and there was no sign of life. The life-boat had difficulty getting back to its station because of engine trouble.

They had only just got ashore when the coast-guard reported he had seen men moving about on the wreck. The boat was unsafe to go out again that day so the engine was overhauled during the night. The next morning the crew returned to the wreck and found sixteen men on it who had been there all the time. They had been shut in the chart house for many hours, having been unable to open the door until the tide subsided. These men had spent the night standing sometimes waist deep in the flooded chart house, and had suffered terribly. When the tide dropped they got out and the coastguard saw them. Every man was saved and Coxswain Smith received a clasp to his silver medal.

When Coxswain Smith retired in 1920, his sight was failing. The long years of strain had told heavily upon him. In 1924, the centenary year of the R.N.L.I., he received the Empire Gallantry Medal from the King at Buckingham Palace. A fellow coxswain had to lead him by the arm as he came out of the palace for his sight had got rapidly worse. He became completely blind, and spent the last years of his life in darkness unable to look upon the sea or his beloved red, blue and white life-boat. But he could still smell the sea and hear its murmuring or its angry roar, and he still had his memories of fifty years spent in the cause of humanity.

On 30th October 1927 Coxswain Robert Smith of Tynemouth died, leaving a name and example that will live for as long as life-boats are needed on the East Coast of Britain.

William Adams of North Deal
1851–1926

Coxswain William Adams of North Deal had stern, strong features. His piercing eyes, hooked nose and short-clipped beard together with his fine bearing made him look the sort of coxswain who would not flinch from any danger. His looks did not deceive, for in courage and seamanship he was a truly great coxswain.

The station at North Deal was responsible for much of the work to the terrible Goodwin Sands, and in almost every great storm there was some urgent call. Occasionally two or three vessels were in distress at the same time, and other life-boats had to help.

For all his arduous labours and hardships in North Sea storms, William Adams lived to the ripe age of seventy-five years. He had been born in 1851, and died in October 1926. Although he joined the life-boat crew as a young man he did not become coxswain until he was fifty-six years old; that was in 1907. He retired after thirteen very active years. During the time he wore the coxswain's life-belt the boat was launched 122 times, saved 321 lives and fourteen ships, mostly from the clutches of the Goodwins. That was a proud record.

Apart from earning the Institution's silver medal three times, Coxswain Adams received two silver medals from foreign governments, and a gold watch from the President of the U.S.A.

The first time he won the silver medal was early in 1916, when he braved the fury of the Sands and succeeded in getting eleven men off the trawler *De La Pole*. He found her with only her bows out of the water. Seven men were in the rigging, three in the fo'c'sle, and the captain was standing waist deep in water on the bridge. The life-boatmen acted promptly. They saved everyone although the captain had to jump into the sea and was dragged into the life-boat almost unconscious.

The same year Coxswain Adams again won the coveted medal. The Italian steamer *Val Salice* was drifting on to the Goodwins, and sent up distress signals. The life-boat had to battle against a hurricane-like wind and was hampered by the thick darkness. It was midnight when the wreck was reached, but by using a searchlight the Deal men got up to her and saved the entire crew of thirty. It was a great feat of seamanship.

That day's record shows what life-boats stationed opposite the Goodwins have to face in a storm; apart from the service by North Deal No. 1 boat already related, the reserve boat had already gone out to another wreck and had returned home after taking an awful beating. It had nearly been capsized three times. The Ramsgate boat had also been to the same wreck in vain, but the Kingsdown boat eventually rescued the crew.

In November 1919 there was no telephone cable from the Goodwin lightships to the shore and they had to signal for aid by firing guns or rockets. It was the booming of the lightships' guns across the stormy sea that called out the Deal boat, *Charles Dibdin*. It took three hours' all-out rowing and sailing for the life-boat to reach the spot where a three-masted schooner, the *Toogo*, was drifting on to the sands. The vessel struck before the Deal men could reach her and almost at once the *Toogo* sank with seven of her crew and a woman still clinging to the rigging which remained above water.

Because of the darkness and the broken water around the wreck the life-boat could not help them. It had to beat about the wreckage hunting for survivors. The life-boat crew repeatedly heard shouts above the roar of wind and the pounding of breakers on the sand, but they could not find anyone. It was most eerie to hear those calls from the blackness where the ship had gone down, and yet for all their searching to find no one. When the dawn came two limp figures were seen hanging on to a capsized boat. All night long they had clutched at that boat hearing the calls from the life-boat crew but unable to guide them. The struggle to get them into the life-boat, helpless and half-dead, was one of the worst Coxswain Adams ever had. After all they had suffered during that night it seemed that the sea was going to claim them as well as all their shipmates. Big waves kept breaking over the life-boat and Coxswain Adams and three others were knocked down and injured. But at last the two men were dragged into the *Charles Dibdin*.

Almost as soon as the crew of the *Charles Dibdin* got back to Deal after that unceasing battle against the storm their boat was needed to go to another wreck. It was again taken out by the reserve crew who only reached the vessel after five hours' backbreaking rowing.

One of the things about that wild night that men along the Kentish coast still remember, although fifty years have passed, is that Coxswain William Stanton of the reserve crew got up from a sick bed to take out the life-boat, knowing that in a day or two he must go into hospital for treatment for a cancer of the throat. He died ten months later. Words cannot do justice to such deeds and such men.

Henry Blogg of Cromer
1876–1954

Henry Blogg of Cromer was the greatest of the great men who pilot Britain's life-boats. The skill, daring and self-sacrifice of the service were consistently shown in him, for his fame does not rest on one or two splendid rescues but on a lifetime of devotion to duty and countless acts of heroism and fine seamanship. No other life-boatman has won so many medals for courage. He won the Institution's gold medal, its highest award, three times; the silver medal, four times; the George Cross and the British Empire Medal; the Queen's Coronation Medal, an Italian medal and a medal from the Canine Defence League. Such a record is unlikely ever to be equalled. When he died, in June 1954, his twelve decorations were carried on a black velvet cushion behind the coffin.

But Henry Blogg left more behind than his medals, he left Cromer life-boat station, and indeed the whole service, an example that has encouraged men to risk their lives in an effort to save life.

Blogg was born in Cromer. He lived and died there. In fact, he was so devoted to life-boat work he rarely left the town in case he should be needed. The great coxswain was a good scholar and when he had learned as much as the school could teach him, he learned all his step-father could teach him about crab, herring and mackerel fishing and seamanship. At the age of eighteen he joined the life-boat crew, and eight years later was elected second coxswain. In his early thirties he became Coxswain Henry Blogg.

His first spectacular rescue took place in January 1917, during World War I. With an elderly crew, for the war had taken the young men, he led the rescue of sixteen men from a Greek ship. He then encouraged and inspired his men, tired as they were, to struggle again and again in the face of a terrible onshore wind to reach the Swedish timber ship *Fernebo*, which hit a mine and blew in halves. If ever men achieved the impossible it was that day. The life-boat was tossed contemptuously back by the huge seas. The men were flung and knocked about, but although half-dead from fatigue and exposure they kept on trying until Henry Blogg noticed an outward-flowing current near a breakwater. He got his boat into it, and reached the wreck. The shipwrecked men were saved and the name of Henry Blogg rang round England. "Those life-boatmen made me proud that I was an Englishman," said one eye-witness.

Ten years later the rescue of fifteen men from the Dutch oil-tanker *Georgia*, which broke in two on the Haisborough Sands, brought the second gold medal. The third came with the magnificent and audacious service to Convoy 559. The first silver medal was won in 1932, when thirty lives were saved from the Italian ship *Monte Nevoso*. The life-boatmen also brought back with the crew several budgerigars and a fine Tyrolean dog that was later given to Henry Blogg and which he christened Monte. In 1933 two men were snatched from the sailing barge *Sepoy* in a rescue that set thousands of people, who had gathered along the front at Cromer, cheering wildly. That was also worth a silver medal as was the saving of twenty-nine men from the Greek vessel *Mount Ida* in 1939, when Blogg had to go to the Ower Bank—thirty miles out from Cromer. The fourth came in 1941, when forty-four men were taken off the *English Trader*.

On this last silver medal service, when the motor life-boat was near the wreck it was rolled on to its beam ends by a great wave, so that the seamen in the *English Trader* actually saw the keel of the life-boat come out of the water. Henry Blogg and four of his crew were washed overboard. Fortunately, the life-boat righted herself, and the remainder of the crew were able to pick up the five men, who were kept afloat by their kapok life-belts. Coxswain Blogg, who was over sixty, suffered greatly from this experience and Signalman E. Allen collapsed and died after being got back into the life-boat. The Cromer men were so exhausted that they could not help the crew of the *English Trader*. They went to Great Yarmouth, where they had to be helped out of their boat, had a meal and changed their clothes. They slept for a few hours and at four o'clock the next morning left Yarmouth, sailed through the wintry darkness in utter silence and rescued the crew of the wreck. Never before had a Cromer life-boatman lost his life and his comrades were grimly determined he should not have died in vain. Such was the spirit that Henry Blogg infused into his crew.

Henry Blogg retired from the service in 1947, aged seventy-one, having been coxswain for thirty-eight years and a member of the crew for fifty-three years. During that time 873 lives had been saved by the Cromer life-boats.

Notwithstanding his great achievements this East Coast fisherman remained humble and unspoilt by the honours he received. It was almost impossible to get him to talk of his deeds; in fact, he was no talker at all. But he did use his voice on the touchline of the football field and in the life-boat. He delighted to watch Cromer play, but was a persistent barracker and nearly burst his lungs yelling abuse and, only very occasionally, encouragement at the players. In the life-boat he also had to shout to drown the noise of the engine and the storm, so that after a service he was often hoarse for days.

Henry Blogg loved children, and at Cromer, where he had a beach-hut hiring business in the summer, he made friends with countless young visitors. He was, however, a dreadful tease and the children he liked most he aggravated most. But many an album has a happy snapshot showing Cromer's famous coxswain with a laughing youngster on either side of him.

Robert Cross of the Humber
1876–1964

When Coxswain Robert Cross retired from the service in 1943 he had won the gold medal twice, the silver medal three times, the bronze medal twice, and the George Medal. He had taken part in the rescue of 403 lives during the thirty-one years he was in command of the Humber life-boat station. He was born in the same month as Henry Blogg.

One of Coxswain Cross's earliest spectacular deeds took place in December 1915, when the Spurn life-boat went out to the S.S. *Florence* which had stranded on the Middle Binks, a stretch of sandbanks off the Humber. It was night, with a gale blowing and a furious sea running on the sands. The life-boat could not get alongside the vessel because of the shallow water, so the coxswain asked for a volunteer to take a line from the boat to the vessel over the sands. No one offered to go as it seemed almost certain death, so Coxswain Cross left his tiller and jumped overboard with a line around his waist. But the seas were too strong for him and he had to be hauled back. It was, however, the only way to save the men on the wreck, and a member of the crew, George Martin, inspired by the coxswain's example, volunteered to go overboard and pay out the line. Standing in the seas by the life-boat George Martin took the strain off the line while his coxswain struggled through the waves and got his end of the line connected to the ship. Robert then helped each seaman back to the life-boat, grasping the rope to steady them. At times he was smothered by the sea, but all the *Florence*'s crew of eight were safely taken in the life-boat.

For this fine deed Coxswain Robert Cross received the silver medal.

He won a bar to this medal in October 1939, shortly after the war had started, in an unusual service to the trawler *Saltaire* which ran aground on the Inner Binks. The crew of nine were all rescued but later, at low tide, they returned to their trawler and endeavoured to save her. While they were on the vessel, however, the sea got up so suddenly that the *Saltaire* was swung round, fell over, and lay at an angle of forty-five degrees with the seas breaking over her. The crew had to take shelter in the wheelhouse, and their position was precarious.

The life-boat again went to their assistance. This time it was an extremely difficult task, for the life-boat could not possibly get alongside; the masts of the *Saltaire,* sticking out like lances, prevented an approach. Although in broken water, Robert Cross and his crew kept their boat riding at anchor for over an hour with such skill that they not only fired a line to the trawler but got block and tackle aboard and hauled seven of the crew by breeches buoy to the life-boat. Not one man was hurt, but the other three men still on the wreck, who had watched their comrades hauled through the water, refused to face that trip through the breaking seas. They preferred to wait for rescue from the shore. They fired a line to the beach and a party of soldiers hauled them ashore through the surf but two of the men were dragged in unconscious and the third had a broken leg.

The service for which Coxswain Cross won his first gold medal and also the George Medal took place less than six months later.

It was in February 1940. The weather was bitterly cold with snow falling and a strong wind blowing. The eerie light of flares had been seen over the sea and the life-boat *City of Bradford II* went out with a crew of only six (one of whom had got up from a sick bed) instead of eight because of illness.

The steam trawler *Gurth* with nine men on board had struck the shore. A tide running across the set of the seas presented the life-boatmen with a problem. Coxswain Cross reached the scene, anchored 150 yards from the ship and dropped down on his cable, stern first. The seas were so heavy that both cock-pits were full for much of the time although the scuppers were gushing continuously. The boat, however, was pushed right out of her course by the tide but the coxswain knew a "rope trick"; by bending a rope from the stern bollard on to his anchor cable he was able to point his bows at the wreck and use his engines to bring his boat up to the *Gurth* for a few seconds at a time. In that moment or two a man might jump or be dragged into the life-boat. Twenty times he did this but had got only six men on board, for it was pitch dark and the boat was frequently lifted too high by the seas for a man to jump into it. The *City of Bradford* was so short-handed there was no one to work the searchlight or relieve the helm, and the mechanic had to manage both engines. He was working with only his chin above water, and the rest of the crew were thrown to the deck time and time again. The boat got plenty of knocking about. In fact, it was amazing that she was not smashed to pieces. To crown their difficulties one of the engines stopped; a rope had been washed overboard and fouled the port propeller. Still Coxswain Cross carried on, despite the added danger, for now the boat steered badly, pulling to one side. "She was like a bird with a broken wing," said the coxswain. Again and again he worked his boat up to the trawler and at last rescued the remainder of the crew.

Then they had to get back out of the surf for they were on a lee shore. The rope from the stern was cut and immediately the life-boat swung into the shallows and bumped on the sands, splitting her rudder and damaging her stern post. It was a critical position. Fortunately, the boat still responded to the helm. Somehow they got out of the broken water and were able to reach the rope fouling the propeller and cut it away with a special knife. Their troubles were ending; with both engines working, they ran for Grimsby. They had been out three and a half hours and had spent ninety minutes in the actual rescue. Folk who helped them to tie up in Grimsby Basin said the life-boatmen were suffering more severely and looked more exhausted than the rescued men—and they were in bad shape. The boat looked like a "battle-scarred warrior".

The Institution described the service as "one of the most difficult and gallant rescues in the history of the Life-boat Service." They added that the coxswain's "courage, endurance and skill were beyond praise."

Just a year later the Humber crew accepted a great hazard in going into mine-strewn waters to investigate rockets that were fired into the dark night during a full gale from the S.S.E. A mine had exploded and a ship was reported sunk. Coxswain Cross ran through an area where German aircraft had been mine-laying the previous day. He found the air raid balloon ship *Thora* aground on Trinity Sands. With wonderful skill he took off her crew of eight men and landed them safely at Grimsby.

For this daring rescue Coxswain Cross received a clasp to his bronze medal.

The second gold medal service came on 6th January 1943, when Coxswain Cross had a hectic time answering repeated calls to vessels in trouble—one of which was the *Almondine*—near the Humber boom defences.

For most of his life Coxswain Cross was an active Sunday School worker and a staunch Methodist. He retired from the life-boat service in December 1943. His record during World War II was packed with drama and danger, and was the greatest in the whole noble service.

Robert Patton of Runswick
1888–1934

In any modern book of golden deeds the story of Coxswain Robert Patton's rescue of a cripple would have a proud place. No finer act of self-sacrifice can be found in the annals of the life-boat service. A man full of health and energy, with a wife, and a daughter still at school; with all the joys and responsibilities of a happy home and a job he loved, gave his life to save a total stranger one February morning out in the North Sea.

Forty-six-year-old Coxswain Robert Patton belonged to a life-boat family. He had been connected with the Runswick

(Yorkshire) boat since 1904, and had helped in the rescue of many men who tried to swim ashore from the wrecked hospital ship *Rohilla*. Altogether he had served for thirty years with the life-boats, excepting a period during the First World War when he had been on mine-sweepers.

His boat, *The Always Ready*, was a new one and had not long been stationed at Runswick. In the dark, early-morning hours of 8th February 1934 she answered a call to help the salvage steamer *Disperser*, which was in grave difficulties because of a gale and heavy seas about five miles out in the North Sea. She had been towed by a tug until her condition became so bad it was certain she would sink. The tug then took seven of the crew of eight safely aboard, but could not save the last man for he was a cripple.

When the motor life-boat reached the scene at 5.30 a.m. she tried, in the darkness, to get near enough to the steamer to take off the remaining man. The sea, however, was so rough that it was impossible, and the *Disperser* sank lower and lower in the water. At last the life-boat seized a chance and came alongside. Her crew yelled wildly to the man who was clinging to the rails of his sinking ship, "Jump for your life!" But the wind was whining and drumming through the ship's rigging and the sea was crashing heavily against her iron sides. Perhaps he did not hear, for he did not jump. Perhaps he heard, but felt he could not jump, being lame. He may have been too overcome with fear to take such perilous action. Instead of jumping, he climbed over the side of the sinking *Disperser*, and hung there. As the life-boat rose on the crest of a wave almost level with the man, Coxswain Robert Patton grabbed him and shouted, "Let go. Let go." But the lame man only clung the tighter.

At that critical moment the life-boat, which was not tied to the steamer, sheered away, and Coxswain Patton felt himself being dragged with it—away from the man he was trying to save. He could release the man, but if he did so the cripple, who had no lifebelt, would drop into the sea and almost certainly be drowned. There was no time for careful thought, it had to be an instant decision and Coxswain Patton made it—he held on! He was dragged over the guard rail and pulled completely out of his boat. The coxswain, however, did not release his hold. He knew his own kapok life-belt was capable of supporting both him and the lame man.

Then the sea, as though determined to prevent this rescue, lifted the life-boat as it would a cork and swung it against the *Disperser*. Coxswain Patton saw the walls of wood and iron closing upon him, but he could do nothing. He was caught between the two vessels and although the kapok life-belt took some of the blow, Coxswain Patton was badly crushed. The cripple was unhurt, being protected by the man holding him. Both men fell into the sea. The crew saw their desperate peril, and leaned right over the gunwale struggling fiercely to get them into the life-boat.

It is extremely difficult to get a heavy man with his clothes weighted by water over the projecting fender of a life-boat, especially if he is wearing a life-belt. It sticks out from his chest and catches under the fender.

"Get him first," gasped Coxswain Patton to his men.

With desperate effort they dragged the lame man out of the sea, but before they could rescue their coxswain the life-boat had twice swung back against the steamer further crushing his body.

At last they got the injured hero into the life-boat, and laid him gently in the cabin. His condition was so serious the crew knew that there was little they could do other than get back home as quickly as possible. They were beside themselves with anxiety. The crew swung the life-boat away from the wreck and drove at full speed for Runswick. When they had got a few hundred yards the steamer rolled right over and sank. The ship was gone, but all her crew had been saved—at a price!

It was 6 a.m. and still dark when *The Always Ready* reached the shore. Coxswain Patton was immediately taken to hospital, but his internal injuries were most severe. Everything that skill and devotion could do was done for him.

On that first day the crew stood about hour after hour awaiting some definite report of their leader. But there was no verdict, his life was in the balance. Day after day passed and hope began to grow that Coxswain Patton would recover. His men clutched eagerly at every hopeful sign. Then the reports of his condition became less promising and the crew knew that Robert Patton would never take them to sea again. Their hearts were unspeakably heavy and yet pride mingled with sadness, for every man who had been out there in the North Sea in the darkness of that winter's morning knew how magnificent had been their coxswain's deed.

When Robert Patton was conscious and able to talk he spoke to an officer of the Institution about the service. He admitted he knew the risk he had run in holding on to the shipwrecked man, but the man was a cripple, without a life-belt, and paralysed with fear by his awful predicament. Coxswain Patton lay quiet for a time as though thinking over the matter afresh, then he added with finality, "I couldn't let the poor lad go. He might have been drowned."

On the ninth day after the rescue Robert Patton died.

Everyone who heard the story was deeply stirred. For miles around and along the whole Yorkshire coast men came to pay tribute to such a hero. Four thousand people assembled at the funeral. Later the Prince of Wales, as President of the R.N.L.I., presented the gold medal to Mrs. Patton. In this case it had been awarded after the coxswain's death as a rare distinction.

As a further honour Runswick's life-boat, *The Always Ready,* was renamed *Robert Patton—The Always Ready.*

Would that space permitted to tell of Thomas Langlands of Whitby; John Swanson of Longhope in the Orkneys, who twice won the silver medal; Edward Wickham of Wexford; John Swan of Lowestoft; William Gammon of the Mumbles; Patrick Murphy of County Down; John McLean of Peterhead; and a score of others whose deeds and work are beyond praise.

7 More Great Rescues

The long record of the life-boat service is made up of countless splendid rescues from shipwreck. They glitter like gems in the bright crown of the Institution. Every station can tell of gallant deeds that thrill the hearer. And it is not always the service to the largest ship or the largest number of lives brought to safety that make the greatest rescues. The mission to the little barge *Sepoy* off Cromer was an epic; the snatching of one man from the *Disperser* off Runswick has no peer.

The following are but a few of the hundreds of rescues that deserve to be called great—rescues that prove man's humanity to man.

THE HOSPITAL SHIP "ROHILLA"

Three months after the beginning of the First World War, on 30th October 1914, the 7,400 ton S.S. *Rohilla* was flung on to the rocky coast near Whitby in Yorkshire. There were 229 people on board; five of them were nurses. Five pulling and sailing and one motor life-boat took part in the repeated efforts to rescue them. So exceptional was this service and so many fine deeds were done that three gold medals were awarded.

The *Rohilla* had been hurriedly changed from a liner into a hospital ship. She was on an errand of mercy, going from Queensferry to Dunkirk in France to bring wounded soldiers back from the battlefields, when a storm wrecked her, and those on board who had set out to help others themselves needed help.

It was an unusually fierce gale which sprang up after midnight and drove the big ship before it. At 4 a.m. with a deafening rending of iron and timbers, the *Rohilla* struck the rocks. Having got the ship at their mercy the seas so hammered it that it broke in two. Scores of men were immediately washed away.

The *Rohilla* lay four to five hundred yards from the shore, hemmed in by rocks against which the waves broke in wild confusion. Distress signals had already been sent up before the ship broke her back. They had been seen by Coxswain Thomas Langlands of Whitby. He at once called out his men, but the seas prevented them launching that night. The oilskin-clad men waited impatiently for the morning. Then, to get as near the wreck as possible, the life-boat *John Fields* was dragged on skids down a steep, rocky bank and hauled over a sea wall, eight feet high. Such a task would have seemed utterly impossible at first sight. It was only the great need of the men on the wreck that gave the launchers the inspiration to attempt such a thing. As was to be expected the life-boat was damaged in doing this, but it was the only way to reach the *Rohilla* in that awful storm. The boat was launched, the crew strained at their oars, and, finding a way through the rocks, reached the broken ship.

The five nurses and a dozen men were hurriedly taken aboard the *John Fields* and brought ashore. Again the boat went to the wreck. This time eighteen men were taken off. During both trips heavy seas repeatedly filled the life-boat. She was low in the water, and many times struck submerged rocks so that after the second voyage it was unsafe to make another attempt.

Coxswain Henry Blogg, G.C., B.E.M., of Cromer

'Coxswain Blogg making rescues from the barge *Sepoy*, 1933, in heavy surf: Cromer church in the background.'
From the painting by Charles Dixon, R.I.

Life-boat designers
and their boats:
J. R. Barnett

52 ft. Barnett boat

R. A. Oakley

48 ft. 6 in. Oakley boat

Launching the Peterhead life-boat

Poster-stamps (1950) illustrating the work of the life-boat service. See pages 180–1.

ROYAL NATIONAL LIFE-BOAT INSTITUTION
1800
The ORIGINAL off Tynemouth Castle
1830
Wreck of ST. GEORGE in Douglas Bay
1881
Ramsgate life-boat & INDIAN CHIEF
1890
A wrecked schooner & Southsea life-boat
1900
Rescue from barque GLIMT: Lizard
Cromer life-boat & wreck of SEPOY
1936
Ballycotton life-boat & Daunt Rock Lightship
1942
Rescue from crashed bomber: Wells, Norfolk
3D
POSTERSTAMPS LTD.
FOUNDER
ROYAL NATIONAL LIFE-BOAT INSTITUTION
6D
LIEUT. COL.
SIR WILLIAM HILLARY, BT
POSTERSTAMPS LTD

Building life-boats at
Messrs Samuel White of Cowes

An urgent call was sent to the *Upgang* pulling and sailing life-boat. To reach the *Rohilla* this boat had to be brought through Whitby town and over the fields. Several horses and hundreds of Whitby people toiled at the task until the heavy boat was brought to the cliff top. Then it had to be lowered by ropes down the cliffs to the beach. Such a herculean labour took many hours, and it was not until 2 p.m. that the boat was ready to launch. The seas, however, were so heavy it was quite impossible to get the boat away. So the *Upgang* men got out of the biting wind and waited for the sea to moderate. But there was no change. After hours of impatient inactivity they saw the darkness fall and knew they could do nothing till morning.

Meanwhile the life-boats at Scarborough and Teesmouth had been summoned. The seas at Scarborough were so furious that neither the life-boat *Queensbury* nor her tug could so much as get out of the harbour. At 3.30 p.m. however, the seas had moderated and the *Queensbury* was towed to the wreck, arriving at 6 p.m. It was then completely dark and the life-boatmen could do nothing but stand by through the night. When daylight came they could not get near the wreck, and had no alternative but to return home.

The Teesmouth life-boat was ready at 2.30 p.m., but as they could not reach the *Rohilla* before darkness set in, it was judged wisest to wait for the new day. At 5 a.m., therefore, she was towed out of the harbour to do what she could for the ship-wrecked men. The seas so battered her, however, that she began leaking. The crew had to be taken on board the tug and everyone returned to Middlesbrough.

Friday had been a fruitless day! The men left on the wreck were growing more and more desperate. Then, at 9 a.m. on Saturday, the *Upgang* crew made another attempt to reach the *Rohilla*. Again they were beaten back. However, they got so close to the ship that the spirits of those on board soared. When they saw her thrown back to the shore black despair settled on many. They jumped into the sea in a wild attempt to save themselves. The strongest swimmers were helpless in such broken water, and although people on the shore rushed into the surf and dragged several to safety, a large number were drowned.

The other Whitby life-boat, with Coxswain Langlands again in command, made yet another attempt. This boat was towed by a tug almost to the wreck, but the murderous seas breaking on the rocks around the *Rohilla* made a barrier they could not cross, and they had to return.

On the decks of the wreck scores of men could be seen huddled together or walking dejectedly about. The life-boat authorities at Whitby were growing increasingly anxious for the fate of those still on the wreck. The need for a motor life-boat was imperative if anyone else was to be saved. The best crews along the coast, pulling until their hearts nearly burst, could not beat the mighty seas. It was not skill nor courage that was lacking, it was sheer power alone to overcome the force of wind and waves. The finest and strongest men at the the oars tired and flagged with their efforts, but the pistons of a petrol engine neither tired nor ached.

The nearest motor life-boat unfortunately was over forty miles away. Yet matters were so desperate the Tynemouth boat was summoned at 4.15 p.m. on Saturday.

Within fifteen minutes the *Henry Vernon* with Coxswain Robert Smith in charge was on her way. Captain H. Burton, a pioneer of motor life-boats, came with the boat to help in the journey to Whitby. Forty-four miles of storm-lashed waters lay between them and the wreck. There were no coastal lights to aid them, for these had been put out because of the war, but the life-boat drove on through the gale fighting every yard of the way to make such an epic rescue that men would say in later years, "Do you remember when the *Henry Vernon* came down from Tynemouth to the *Rohilla*?"

It took all the seamanship the Tynemouth men knew and all

the strength they could summon to keep the boat on its course in the face of such waves. They were in constant danger of being washed overboard when the boat took "green" seas on board. Somehow they stuck it and just after midnight the *Henry Vernon* reached Whitby. Oil was at once taken on board to calm the water around the wreck.

After a few hours' rest—at six o'clock on Sunday morning—Coxswain Smith made his rescue bid. He took his boat to windward of the *Rohilla* and poured the oil upon the sea so that the tide carried it around the wreck. The effect of those few gallons of oil was magical. As it spread, the churned waters subsided in an amazing way. It was as though a frenzied animal was suddenly calmed. Then, with propeller turning at full speed, the life-boat dashed back and got in the lee of the wreck, almost, as it were, before the sea realized it was about to be cheated of its prey.

Forty men, numb and stiff from exposure, scrambled down a rope ladder into the life-boat in half as many minutes. The boat was almost too crowded for the crew to work but there were still ten men on the wreck. They were hanging over the rail when two mountainous waves were seen from the shore bearing rapidly down on the *Rohilla*. Hundreds of people cried a warning as the two masses of water moved swiftly, one after the other, towards the wreck. It was as though the sea had sent them to crush this attempt at rescue. They swept over the halved wreck, right over the bridge, and tumbled in mighty power upon the life-boat. She was smothered by tons of green water. Once, twice, she disappeared completely, with every man grimly clutching some part of the life-boat. They could do nothing to avoid those terrible waves.

The hundreds of watchers on the shore groaned in anguish, believing that all had been lost, but from out of the heaving waters the *Henry Vernon* reappeared, staggering under her great load of water and humanity but still afloat. She rolled, as if shaking herself free, then steadied. When Coxswain Smith checked up, expecting at least a dozen men had been swept away, not one was missing. His relief was too great for words.

He would not leave the other ten men on the wreck as the risk of any further attempt was so great, but kept his boat alongside until they too had tumbled on to his decks.

Every man was at last off the ship and fifty rescued men were crowded in the motor boat. The last man to come down the swaying rope ladder was the *Rohilla*'s captain, and as he jumped into the life-boat a cheer went up from the shore. The North Sea had not got all the victims it sought.

All, however, was not yet over; as the laden boat fought her way back to the shore a roaring breaker hit her. She rolled over, over, almost on to her beam-ends before righting herself and struggling on. Again, miraculously, no one was lost.

That was the sea's last attempt to stop the rescue. The *Henry Vernon* reached the shore and behind her the once proud but now broken *Rohilla* was left to be a plaything for the waves. More precious, however, even than the fine ship were the eighty-five lives that had been saved after enduring so much. The tragedy was that two-thirds of the people on board that vessel of mercy had perished.

Most of the survivors were barefooted and many were dressed only in pyjamas. They had not been able to get their clothes from the flooded cabins and, scantily clad, had endured fifty hours of exposure in that fierce storm. They were blue with cold, shivering violently, and had been without food and drink for two days. How the crowds welcomed and cheered them. Eager hands gave them warm clothes and food. Only when they had been warmed and fed were they allowed to tell the story of their suffering and the despair that had gripped them as they had watched so many brave but unsuccessful attempts to rescue them.

There was one survivor from the wreck not shown on the official records—a black kitten which a seaman brought ashore sitting on his shoulder. All through his own ordeal he had protected the little creature.

The R.N.L.I. awarded its gold medal to Coxswains Robert Smith and Thomas Langlands, and also to Captain Burton.

The outstanding superiority of the motor life-boat was clearly demonstrated, and the policy of installing them wherever possible was greatly strengthened.

THE KETCH "EXCEL"

Moelfre is on the east side of the Isle of Anglesey. It is a small, little-known place but on the night of 28th October 1927 its life-boat won lasting renown in a grand service to the *Excel*, a two-masted sailing ship called a ketch.

Fierce gales swept across southern Ireland, Wales and England at the end of October. In some places, including Holyhead, gusts reached hurricane force. There was much loss of life at sea and calls from distressed vessels brought out seventeen life-boats. Irish fishermen from villages in the lonely islands of County Mayo and Galway were using open rowing boats, some fishing even in canvas-covered coracles. They were caught by the tempest and overwhelmed. Fifty men lost their lives.

The gales were at their worst on 28th and 29th and nine pulling and sailing life-boats were launched from Lancashire and North Wales during those days. The first was the Moelfre boat, with Second-Coxswain William Roberts in charge and Captain Jones assisting him. A vessel was in trouble three miles from Point Lynas lighthouse, on the north-east corner of the island. It was then three o'clock in the afternoon of the 28th and it took over two hours to reach the ship, for the gale was at its peak and it was bitterly cold.

The crew found the *Excel* moored to a German steamer which had gone to her help and had stopped her from drifting. They were unable to take off the crew, however, owing to the violent waves. When the life-boat arrived the Germans cut the mooring rope thinking the life-boatmen could then complete the rescue. But with the rope cut the *Excel* lurched away before the wind, and the Moelfre boat could not get alongside her. The sailing ship rolled and pitched, rapidly filling with water. It looked as if she would sink at any moment. There was no time to lose. Coxswain Roberts consulted Captain Jones and decided that it would be too late to help unless they took the desperate course of running their life-boat on top of the sinking ketch and snatching off her crew. The risks were only too plain—it would certainly damage the life-boat, and might even wreck it. They might fail to save the three men on the sailing ship, and also lose their own lives. The darkness added to the danger, but there was no other way. The crew listened grimly as the coxswain yelled his intention above the noise of the storm and then nodded assent. They, too, accepted the risk.

The life-boat was brought to windward of the wreck, the rudder was swung round and the bows pointed at the dark shape of the wallowing *Excel.* Coxswain Roberts gave the order and partly under sail the life-boat was lifted by a great wave above the waterlogged ketch and carried on to her upper deck. The three men on board were desperate; they scrambled, or were hurriedly hauled in the darkness, into the life-boat. As they fell among the life-boatmen another wave lifted the boat and swept it off the drowning ketch.

Three large holes had been knocked in the hull of the Moelfre boat. Worse still, when one of the three men was being dragged into the life-boat he was so severely injured that he died soon after. In the confusion and the darkness no one knew how he was hurt, or even when he died. But when the boat at last reached the shore he was found to be dead.

The *Excel* did not last much longer. A towering wave swept over her; the stern rose; the masts with their tattered sails quivered at a steep angle, then went beneath the waves. The

German steamer went on its way thinking the rescue was over. It was far from over for the life-boatmen; in fact, this was but the beginning of what has seemed to them ever since a hideous nightmare.

Water had poured into the damaged life-boat and she could not ride the breakers, but ploughed heavily into them. To make matters worse her jib sail was ripped to tatters and she could not sail properly. The crippled life-boat was heavy to handle. They had rescued the crew of the *Excel* but were themselves in grave danger. A struggle now began to reach the shore. The only thing the damaged boat could do was make for the Menai Straits where she would find some shelter from the storm. Could she get there? That was to be the test, and their lives depended on it. The cold and the flaying wind tried the endurance of that tough crew. They were used to storms but this was worse than anything they had known. Many times they almost despaired of reaching the shore. Their minds grew as numb as their bodies. The night wore slowly on in intense physical effort, pulling at the big oars and trying to control the damaged boat and keep her from taking the seas too heavily. So awful was the struggle that one of the crew, also named William Roberts, collapsed and died from exertion and exposure.

Hour after hour the fight went on until the half-dead men realized as though in a dream that they must be getting near the Straits and shelter. At 2 a.m., having covered nearly twenty miles from the wreck, the crew knew the seas were less violent and somehow they had reached calmer waters. They anchored near Puffin Island. Every man had reached the absolute limit of endurance. They just lay in the bottom of the boat like dead men. Coxswain Roberts and Captain Jones were themselves too overcome to assist anyone else. They had only enough strength to stay at the helm and keep the life-boat head-on to the seas.

Ashore there was growing uneasiness about the fate of the

life-boat. The gale was so violent that as the hours passed without news or sign of the boat, a disaster was feared. The coastguard at Beaumaris, who had been keeping ceaseless watch for signals as all the telephone wires were down, was informed by messenger of the anxiety at Moelfre. He immediately told the local coxswain and the Beaumaris motor life-boat was launched. She hunted around in the darkness of the gale for signs of the missing boat. The search was unrewarded, so the coxswain went to the Menai Straits where he guessed the Moelfre men would seek shelter. Close to Puffin Island they at last saw the life-boat anchored. Then, when the suffering of the Moelfre men might have been shortened, one of those strange things happened that can never be properly explained. The life-boat was found, but the Beaumaris men assumed that as it was in comparative shelter all was well and no assistance was needed. They turned and went home without even hailing the pulling and sailing life-boat. Back at Beaumaris they reported they had found the Moelfre boat safely anchored in the Straits!

On board the anchored boat the crew were still so exhausted they were unable to help themselves. When aid failed to come they could only remain at anchor and wait for the morning.

With the new day people on the shore saw the Moelfre boat still at anchor and showing no sign of activity. They realized all was not well. The motor life-boat was again sent out and once more found the Moelfre boat. As they came close the pitiful plight of her crew and the men she had saved was only too apparent. Without delay they put men on board, fixed a tow rope and brought the battered boat into Beaumaris.

It was past 8 a.m. when they reached Beaumaris. The Moelfre men had been out seventeen hours. During that time Second-Coxswain William Roberts had been at the tiller without a break. So severe had been his ordeal that he was completely blind for many hours from the lashing of the wind and the effects of the salt water as well as the strain of that night.

Captain Jones had assisted him in every way he could. Every member of the crew needed medical aid and none was able to work for a week. Some had to rest for two or three weeks to recover. Even in the life-boat service, where crews are called to go out in the worst of weather, few men have had to endure such an ordeal.

In recognition of their courage and suffering the Institution awarded its gold medal to Second-Coxswain William Roberts and Captain Owen Jones, and its bronze medal to each member of the crew. The widow of William Roberts, who had died doing his duty, received the bronze medal and a pension.

Most of the heroic Moelfre crew had been taught at Llanallgo Council School; some had only left a year or two before, so that when they received an invitation from the head teacher and scholars to visit their old school they went gladly. The teacher told the school the story of that great rescue. The crew was given a supper, and the scholars went home feeling proud that their school had produced heroes whose names had not only gone round Wales, but the whole world.

DAUNT ROCK LIGHTSHIP

The saving of eight men from the Daunt Rock lightship has been described as "one of the most exhausting and courageous rescues in the history of the life-boat service". That is no exaggeration. In the sixty-three hours that the Ballycotton life-boatmen were on the service they slept only three hours and the conditions they had to face were appalling. And it was not merely endurance that was needed, for only by risking their lives again and again were they able to save the men of the light-vessel.

The lightship, just off the south coast of Ireland, warned shipping of the deadly Daunt Rock. The village of Ballycotton was twelve miles away.

On Friday, 7th February 1936, south-easterly gales swept

southern Ireland and raged for days. On Monday the 10th, winds of almost hurricane force were tearing across land and sea. Old men who had spent their lives in Ballycotton could not recall worse tempests. Blocks of masonry weighing a ton were torn by tremendous seas from the harbour and tossed about like a child's bricks. It was difficult to stand in exposed places, and the life-boat at its moorings had to be secured by extra ropes to avoid being dashed against the breakwater. On the land, trees were uprooted, telephone wires brought down, tiles ripped off houses, and hoardings blown over.

The coxswain and crew of the Ballycotton life-boat expected to be called out at any hour. Their own boats in the harbour were in danger of being smashed and required ceaseless watching.

After being up all Monday night securing the coxswain's motor boat, news was received by a messenger, as the telephone wires were down, that the Daunt Rock lightship had broken adrift and was being pushed towards the shore by the wind and the waves.

So fearful were the seas that the secretary of the local life-boat branch told Coxswain Patrick Sliney he would not order him to launch his boat and doubted if the life-boat could even be reached at its moorings. The coxswain heard the news without comment, then walked away with head down towards the harbour.

A little later the secretary followed, expecting to find the coxswain studying conditions to see if there was any likelihood that they might moderate. To his amazement he saw the life-boat plunging into seas at the harbour mouth. The crew had been standing by at the harbour and without an order or firing the maroons Coxswain Sliney had set out. It was about 8.30 a.m. and the men had been on the quay and without sleep all night. But that did not stop them!

The secretary watched spellbound as the life-boat, *Mary Stanford*, left the comparative shelter of the harbour and great seas struck her. One moment the boat was standing almost on its stern climbing a wave and the next it was completely hidden in a trough. As she passed the lighthouse, spray from the breakers was flying over the lantern 196 feet high! Such was the setting for this rescue.

Not one of the crew had ever known the sea in a mood like this. Once or twice their boat dropped into the trough of a wave with such a crash that they expected every timber had been sprung. But she shook herself like a cat that has fallen from a height, and plunged on. The crew, huddled in the rear cockpit, gripped the boat as each wave swept down upon them. Again and again the cockpit was filled, and the scuppers were continually spouting.

Leaving the lighthouse behind, the life-boat took a hazardous short cut between two reefs. This manoeuvre saved them taking a wide circuit and brought them into the open sea. For six miles the *Mary Stanford* ran before the wind but the following seas made the boat so difficult to manage the coxswain ordered the drogue to be thrown out. They slowed down to do this, and in doing so the coxswain was hit by several powerful overtaking seas and knocked almost unconscious. But they got the drogue drawing behind, and it slowed the life-boat, making her more manageable.

Rain was falling and the air was also filled with spume, making visibility poor. They could not find the drifting lightship, although they searched for a dozen miles. There was only one thing to do—go to Queenstown for information. The drogue had been lost so they used the oil sprays to calm the water to get into Queenstown harbour. There they were told the position of the lightship and set out into the wild sea again.

They found the Daunt Rock lightship at midday. She had made doubtful anchorage, and the destroyer *Tenedos* was standing by. The eight men on the lightship, however, did not want to leave their vessel, feeling she was a danger to shipping, since she was miles out of her proper position. They therefore asked the Ballycotton men to keep close at hand.

The destroyer attempted during the afternoon to pass cables to the lightship to take it in tow, but failed. It was nearly dark when they gave up the attempt, and prepared to keep station by the lightship through the night. The life-boat returned to Queenstown for food.

At Ballycotton the people were still trying to find out what had happened to their boat. The secretary was out during the day struggling along tree-obstructed roads beside the shore in an effort to locate the life-boat and maintain communication. Eventually he got in touch with the coxswain at Queenstown and took a new drogue, ropes, and dry clothing for his men twenty-three miles away.

A few of the crew got some sleep that night before the boat went out on Wednesday for its third trip to the lightship. They stood by in more moderate but still rough seas throughout that day and night. When dawn came on Thursday the 13th, the lifeboat had to go back to Queenstown for petrol, food and more dry clothes. The blocked roads prevented the boat from being refuelled until 4 p.m. but once more the Ballycotton boat returned to its duty by the lightship. It was nearly nightfall when they arrived and the seas were getting rougher every minute. One mass of water rushed upon the light-vessel and smothered her from end to end. It tore away fittings of every description but left the half-drowned crew still on their boat. The *Isolda*, a vessel of the Irish Lights, had also arrived and was waiting nearby to take the Daunt Rock ship in tow if the storm abated. By ten o'clock the lightship was bucking like a bronco at the end of her cable and her crew, with life-belts on, were huddled in the stern. Their peril was increasing, for the anchor was dragging and the wind, which had shifted to the S.S.E., was now pushing the lightship slowly but remorselessly towards the Daunt Rock until it was less than a hundred yards away. Coxswain Sliney reported the vessel's danger to the *Isolda* and was told to take off the eight men on board—if he could!

So, after all those hours of battling with the storm, they were now to be supremely tested. Every man was exhausted, numb with cold and suffering from spending hours in soaked clothes. The one thing they wanted was rest and food, not this new ordeal. "If they could." That was the challenge, for the lightship men were in peril of their lives.

The light-vessel was not only plunging at the end of her anchor cable, but her stern was swinging about like a flail. There was only one chance—to run in, check the engines, get the men to jump from the lightship and then back away. Coxswain Sliney decided he would try this, and warned the men on the imperilled ship to be ready to jump, two or more at a time, when he dashed in.

First he released oil around the lightship, but the tide was running so fast this did not have the effect he had hoped. From astern Coxswain Sliney raced his boat alongside the rolling ship and then checked her. As he did so one of the men jumped and landed safely. The engines were reversed and the life-boat withdrew. The second run was fruitless, for no one dared to jump. The third time, however, was more favourable and five men leapt on to the life-boat's deck. Again the manoeuvre must be repeated, for two men still remained. As the *Mary Stanford* dashed alongside, the lightship suddenly lurched and crashed on to her, pushing her down and away. The rails and deck of the life-boat were badly damaged, but by a miracle the life-boat was not capsized and no one was hurt.

Again the run was made without result; the two men on the ship seemed unable to face the risk of jumping. Coxswain Sliney sent some of his crew into the bows and told them to grab the two panic-stricken men. For the sixth time he ran alongside the lightship and as he did so the two men were seized and dragged into the life-boat. In doing so, one was badly cut about the face and the other about the legs, but they were both safely in the life-boat.

The coxswain reported to the *Isolda* that he had now got the eight men and turned for Queenstown. As they started home one of the rescued men became hysterical. The strain of the last few days had been too much and he had to be restrained. Both injured men were given first aid and when they landed at Queenstown at 11 p.m. were taken to hospital.

The *Mary Stanford* remained at Queenstown that night and went home the next morning, arriving at 12.45 p.m. on the 14th.

For this service Coxswain Patrick Sliney received the gold medal, the second coxswain and motor mechanic the silver medal, and each of the crew the bronze medal. Letters of congratulation came in from many parts of the world.

8 Life-boat Disasters

> "Greater love hath no man than this, that a man lay down his life for his friends."
>
> These men went further—they laid down their lives for total strangers.

Although the Institution has spared neither money nor thought to make British and Irish life-boats as safe as possible, the very nature of their work means that the boats must ride with danger. They have to launch when conditions are at their worst and go into places which even the most foolhardy sailor would avoid. It is their job. They go out a hundred, perhaps two hundred, times and fine seamanship and fine boats bring them home safely, but on the very next service disaster may overwhelm them. In the long history of the service most stations have mourned some tragedy to their boats. Lives have been laid down that lives might be saved. That is the price. Sometimes one man is swept from the boat by a wave; sometimes an entire crew is lost when a boat capsizes or is tossed on to the rocks.

To appreciate the risks the life-boatmen run in the course of their work the following disasters are recalled.

The earliest, and one of the worst disasters, took place at the mouth of the Tyne in 1849 when the *Providential* capsized and of her double-banked crew of twenty-four only four were saved.

Twelve years later a hurricane struck the N.E. coast and nine vessels were wrecked off Whitby alone. Yet the Whitby life-boat rescued all the crews except one man. As the Whitby boat came back from her first service she was told of another and went out again. Six times she put out and on the last trip the boat capsized. Of her magnificent, but by this time utterly exhausted, crew only one was saved. That same day, however, when two more distress calls came in together, a fresh crew stepped forward, manned an old life-boat, and saved all the ship-wrecked men.

FETHARD DISASTER

Until calamity struck it on 20th February 1914 few people had heard of Fethard, the small village in the south-west corner of Ireland in County Wexford. Its life-boat, *Helen Blake*, on an errand of mercy, was smashed like an egg-shell against the rocks and nine men perished.

The Norwegian schooner *Mexico* (the same name as in the St. Anne's disaster) was bringing mahogany from America to Liverpool when a storm upset navigation and the ship's officers lost their bearings. They sailed by mistake into Bannow Bay, then, realizing their error, tried to turn about, but the powerful currents and the force of the storm thwarted them and drove the ship almost on to the shore.

The Fethard life-boatmen, seeing the struggles of the sailing vessel to avoid shipwreck, launched their boat to help. They pulled desperately hard at their oars, but before they reached the *Mexico* the schooner hit the rocks.

The life-boat manoeuvred to get near and had got very close to the ship when a wave rose, broke into the life-boat

Princess Marina, Duchess of Kent, President, R.N.L.I. 1943–68, with Coxswain Richard Evans at Moelfre, 1960

The Duke of Kent at Bembridge, Isle of Wight

Goblet, over 12 inches high,
engraved by Honoria D. Marsh.
Acquired in 1964 by the Calouste
Gulbenkian Foundation, Lisbon,
to benefit the R.N.L.I.

Queen Elizabeth II, with Commander F. R. H. Swann, Chairman, R.N.L.I. and (*right*) Lieutenant-Commander W. G. Dutton, Chief Inspector of Life-boats, at Henley, July 1972, on board the *Royal British Legion Jubilee* life-boat

Captain Nigel Dixon, R.N., Secretary, R.N.L.I.

Young members of the Blue Peter team, with records of lives saved by Blue Peter life-boats

The Fraserburgh life-boat (*background*) at the moment of capsize, 21 January 1970

Modern life-boat types: 70 ft. Clyde, steel

44 ft. Waveney, steel

McLachlan Inshore Life-boat

Inshore Life-boat

Commemorative medals, designed by John Crittenden and issued by Messrs Slade Hampton, to signalize the 150th anniversary in 1974 of the founding of the R.N.L.I.

and instantly filled her. The *Helen Blake* rolled under the load of water and the alarmed crew immediately dropped anchor fearing they too would be thrown ashore. But it was too late, the anchor did not hold, and the *Helen Blake* was caught by a huge sea; it was as though a giant hand grasped the life-boat and hurled her against the rocks where she was soon pounded to matchwood. There were fourteen men on board when this happened. Nine were flung overboard and swept away, the other five somehow got on to the rocks, and in a mad scramble over the slimy weed-covered stones escaped beyond the reach of the thundering seas.

They found themselves on an island consisting of bare rocks, but with a few stretches of coarse grass. There was neither bush, tree nor shelter from the winter's wind.

Despite their own experience these five men, battered and racked by grief at the loss of their comrades, at once set to work to try and help the crew of the schooner.

Eight men of the *Mexico* still remained on board, for two had already got ashore in a boat. With the help of ropes the life-boatmen managed to reach and rescue all eight. There were now thirteen ship-wrecked men on the barren island. They were out of reach of the sea, but suffering from cold and shock.

On the mainland watchers had seen through binoculars the calamity that had befallen their life-boat. They could distinguish the survivors moving about on the island and realized that help was urgently needed. The Dunmore life-boat, which was nearest, was called out and tried to reach the castaways, but in spite of repeated attempts and taking grave risks themselves they achieved nothing.

News of the disaster and the peril of the survivors had already been sent to the Institution's headquarters. The Chief Inspector of Life-Boats, Commander Holmes, set out at once for Fethard. On arriving many hours later he found that all attempts to reach the men had failed, and at once went out in the Dunmore boat and organized further efforts but without success. The seas breaking in fury on the tumbled rocks defied their skill and courage to make a landing. The sea held the whip hand.

Two more life-boats, the Kilmore and Wexford, battled along the coast to help. The first boat made three attempts that day and the next without success. The Wexford boat, *Jane Stevens*, was towed to the scene and arrived at 2 p.m. on the 21st. She could not get near the threatened men and at last took refuge in Waterford River, for night was approaching and the storm again increasing.

Meanwhile on the island, the men were in a pitiable plight and the night added to their misery. The gale grew worse until nothing like it had been known in those parts for years. The fierce wind that rocked the Wexford boat perilously, even in the river, cut into the marooned men, who huddled together for warmth and shelter. The icy spray drove over them continuously and their only food, two small tins of meat, had long since gone as had the wine the captain of the *Mexico* had brought ashore with him. A Portuguese sailor was in the worst condition. He had long since ceased moaning and seemed to have passed into a merciful coma. He died before the long-awaited dawn came.

That Sunday was the worst the castaway men and their relatives on the shore had ever known. The sea abated but little and no further rescue attempt could be made.

On Monday, at 6 a.m., the Dunmore life-boat made yet another effort with the Chief Inspector on board. The sea had gone down considerably but conditions were still bad. The boat reached a spot a hundred yards from the rocks and fired a rocket line to the men on the island. The line was taken and a light skiff, which the life-boat had brought along, was tied to it and hauled to the shore. It was almost within grasp of the castaways when a wave smashed it on the rocks. The line was used, however, to haul two men by life-buoy through the surf, but the remainder would not make the risky attempt.

The Wexford life-boat had now arrived towing a stout punt with her. Two men volunteered to work this punt ashore, keeping a line attached to the life-boat. It was a dangerous business, but they were successful and got two men from the island to the life-boat. By making four trips they rescued the remaining ten men.

Their resourcefulness was shown on the second trip when the punt was banged on the rocks and a hole stove in it through which the water poured. Almost as quick as the sea, the life-boatmen grabbed a loaf of bread and some packing and rammed this hard into the hole. It could not be called a neat or permanent repair, but it enabled them to complete their job. When all the men, haggard-eyed and stiff-limbed, were at last in the life-boat the tug hauled them to Fethard where their anxious families had been hoping and praying from 3 p.m. on Friday until 10 a.m. on Monday—sixty-seven hours—for their rescue.

The Fethard disaster stirred seamen and landsmen throughout the British Isles and also in Norway. A fund was immediately raised to help the dependants of the men who had given their lives.

THE CAPSIZING OF THE RYE BOAT

The Rye Harbour life-boat disaster was the worst known there. The entire crew of seventeen was lost, which meant almost all the adult fishermen of that village. The life-boat station had to be closed for there was no one to form a new crew. Perhaps the saddest thing was that only five minutes after the life-boat had gone out a message was received saying it was no longer needed! Had the crew seen the recall signal the disaster need never have happened.

At 6.45 a.m. on 15th November 1928 the pulling and sailing life-boat *Mary Stanford* was called out to help the *Alice*, a Latvian steamer which was drifting in the English Channel and being blown by a south-west gale towards Dungeness. Squalls of rain and a fierce wind buffeted launchers and crew as the boat was shot from its carriage into the surf. Coxswain Herbert Head was at the helm. His men pulled with might and main through the breakers to clear the harbour.

When the message came through to the coastguard that the crew of the *Alice* had been picked up by another steamer the recall signal was fired. Three times it shot up into the dark, stormy sky. But the crew did not see it. Their vision was obscured by spray. They had got the sail up and were busy at their tasks. The all-important message had come too late, and the men continued on their course not knowing their efforts must be in vain.

On the shore, relatives and friends saw the day break, and continued waiting with collars turned up, beating their arms and stamping their feet in the biting wind. The hours dragged past. The thunder of the breakers never diminished, and still the watchers kept peering out across the waters to where they thought the boat would first appear out of the grey haze of lowering clouds and spindrift. Suddenly an excited cry went up, "Look, look, there she is!"

Anxiously men and women screened their eyes from the wind and rain to get a glimpse of their boat. Following the pointing fingers they saw a small sail, dark against the greyness of the sky, but blurred by the smother of spray. It was the life-boat coming back. With sail set and the gale pushing her along the *Mary Stanford* rapidly drew near the shore. The tide was at the flood. Folk crowded to the water's edge ready to help the men ashore, for the boat was now approaching the harbour mouth. The heavy following seas and the wind, blowing in fierce gusts, made this last part of the voyage a tricky business. But these men knew the harbour and the ways of the sea. They had weathered many a storm in their fine boat. It was so close the watchers could see the faces of the men under their yellow sou'westers. It was a relief after the long wait to know the men were back home—the boat was now entering the harbour. Some of the women hurried to their homes to have something hot ready for their men after that exhausting mission. The head launcher was preparing the skeats to get the boat back on its carriage. Everyone on the shore knew their crew had had the long struggle in vain, and were wondering what they would say on being told that the signal had been fired when they were less than a quarter of a mile out. It was at that moment when they were so near to home and safety that disaster overwhelmed the boat.

In a fraction of a minute the whole life of Rye Harbour was changed. The groups of drenched spectators were horrified to see the *Mary Stanford* hit by a monstrous wave and tipped over like a navvy's wheelbarrow. The screams of the watchers rose above the roar of the storm. One moment they saw the life-boat breasting a breaker with spray flying like smoke over her from stem to stern, and her sail billowing with the wind's force; the next she was bottom up with mast and red-brown sails under the water and her crew spilled out into the sea. It happened just as quickly as that. The incoming breakers swept the gleaming white hull towards the shore and many of the crew also. The frantic watchers plunged into the sea and made superhuman efforts to reach the life-boatmen and haul them out of the surf. Six men were thus dragged ashore, but not one was alive. Two of the crew were trapped under the boat.

Seventeen men who had gone out in the storm to save other men had perished—almost on their own doorstep. A pall of sorrow fell upon the village and saddened the whole country.

An inquiry held by the Board of Trade investigated the calamity, especially seeking to discover why the kapok life-belts did not keep the men alive for the short distance they had to go to reach the beach. But no fault was found in the equipment. One benefit did result, however, from the disaster; in future all messages recalling life-boats which had been launched were to be given the same priority over the telephone lines as messages calling them out. Hitherto, such messages had no priority and had to wait their turn.

A national fund was immediately started to provide for the many dependants of the life-boatmen, and money came in generously from all over the country. It was an expression of the sympathy a whole nation felt for those who had lost so much on that black day, 15th November 1928.

THE ST. IVES LIFE-BOAT IS FLUNG ASHORE

St. Ives in Cornwall is not very far from Land's End. The town itself is sheltered from the Atlantic storms, but its life-boat has to leave the sheltered part of the bay and face the full fury of the sea. On 23rd January 1939 the country was shocked to hear that the St. Ives life-boat had been wrecked and one man only of her crew of eight had been saved. The news seemed the worse because the previous year there had also been a disaster at this station and although none of the life-boat crew was lost, five of the twenty-three men they had rescued were drowned.

It was 2 a.m. when the coastguard reported a ship in danger two miles from Cape Cornwall. What ship it was has never been proved, but it is now thought to have been the 3,000 ton steamer *Wilston* which had left Newport two days before and was never seen again. A gale was blowing from the Atlantic. The nearest life-boat was at Sennen Cove, but it could not be launched owing to the low state of the tide. The St. Ives boat was eleven miles from the distressed ship, but when Coxswain Thomas Cocking heard that the Sennen boat could not be launched, he simply said, "We're off", and went to assemble his crew by signal.

Although it was half past two on a January morning, eighty launchers hurried through the storm and darkness to the boathouse to get the boat into the sea. It was away before 3 a.m. A little more than an hour later the coastguard at Clodgy

Point, north of St. Ives, saw red flares light up the darkness well out at sea. They came from the life-boat and meant, "More help needed."

The coastguard took prompt action and sent the St. Ives rocket apparatus round St. Ives Bay to Godrevy Point. He also sent a message to Penlee life-boat which was thirty miles away on the south coast, near Penzance. The Penlee crew set out at 5 a.m. to fight the gale all the way round the end of England.

Meanwhile the St. Ives boat (a reserve boat placed there after the last disaster) had run into great difficulties. As soon as the St. Ives headland was cleared the boat met the gale head-on and great seas flung themselves at her in quick succession. The life-boat had only gone three miles when the first mishap occurred. She topped a big sea but when descending into the trough suddenly sheered. The next sea, close on the heels of the other, hit the life-boat on the starboard bow and instantly capsized her. It was like a punch from a giant. The boat was self-righting and when she turned turtle the engine automatically cut out. The boat did what she was designed to do, and in a matter of seconds was right way up, but Coxswain Cocking, the bowman, the signalman, and one of the crew were missing. The remaining four men, dazed and bruised, first cut away some gear which had been partly washed out of the boat, in case it fouled the propeller. The mechanic then started the engine, but when he put it into gear it stalled. He tried again and again with the same result—something was stopping the propeller from turning!

The anchor was then dropped and the four men tried to hoist the sail to keep the boat's head to the seas, but they could not do it. It needed all the crew to do that job in such a wind. So they burned red flares to tell of their plight and saw the coastguard's answering rocket from Clodgy Point.

In that wild sea the strain on the anchor cable was terrific and although it was new it eventually parted. The life-boat lurched away before the gale, completely at the mercy of the seas—drifting across St. Ives Bay to a shore where the pitiless rocks waited. The mechanic repeatedly got the engine going, but it would not turn the propeller. If only they could have got the engine into gear they would have been saved.

They had been driven several miles by the wind when the almost inevitable happened—the boat again capsized. This time, when it righted itself the mechanic had gone. One of the three men now left, William Freeman, was under the canopy when the boat turned over. The air under the canopy kept out the water, and when he was upside down under the sea his face was not in the water.

The three men were helpless to stop the boat heading towards the rocks. They got in the stern thinking it would give them the best chance when they hit the shore. But they knew that their chances of surviving were very small.

Holding tightly to the cabin rail the bowman saw a terrific sea sweeping upon them. He yelled his warning, "Look out, a big sea's coming!"

The three men could only grip the rail more tightly. The sea hit the helpless boat and for the third time turned her over. When she righted herself, letting out through all her scuppers the hundreds of gallons of seawater that the sea had hurled in, only William Freeman was left!

Alone in an unmanageable boat in that riotous sea! He clung to a rail under the canopy until he heard the thunder of seas crashing on the shore. He knew that in a few minutes the boat would be upon the rocks. They were terrible moments for him as he realized his peril. So far he had lived while every man with whom he had set out had perished, but could he hope to survive the coming shock? The tumult of the breakers grew louder until it was deafening. He felt a sea lift the boat, poise it, and then throw it with a shattering crash upon the boulders of the shore. William Freeman was flung against the side of the canopy with a force that partially stunned him, but he retained sufficient presence of mind to scramble out of the boat, which landed on its side on a ledge of rock. He dropped into the turbulent receding water up to his knees and tried desperately to get as high as possible up the shore. The rocks under his feet were slippery. He feared the next wave would claw him back into the sea. He heard a breaker crash down behind him. The swirling, foaming water caught him. It rushed around him, pushing, clutching and trying to pull him down. But William Freeman kept his feet. As the sea dropped back he staggered further out of the waves' reach. Gasping and sobbing with exertion he dragged himself up a gap in the cliff, slipping and clawing till he reached the top. Then he stumbled on through the early-morning darkness to where he could see a light. It came from a window at Godrevy Farm, standing high and bleak, overlooking the sea. Bruised and battered, with his oil-skins torn to ribbons, he staggered to the door and banged upon it. Farmer Delbridge opened the door and stood amazed at the sight of the drenched, bleeding stranger sagging against his doorpost. He helped Freeman indoors and listened to his incoherent story of the disaster. Calling his wife to help, Mr. Delbridge bound up the life-boatman's cuts, gave him warm drinks and got him to bed. He then cycled through the gale to the nearest telephone and called a doctor. He also rang the St. Ives coastguard and told him of the tragedy.

It was about 7 a.m. and was the first news the anxious folk of St. Ives had received of their men who four hours earlier had set out to help an unknown ship. The headquarters of the R.N.L.I. were immediately informed and soon the whole country knew of the disaster that had overtaken these brave men while most of the people of England slept safely in their beds.

The Penlee life-boat had nearly reached the Longships lighthouse when the Land's End coastguard learned of the St. Ives disaster. He at once signalled her that she was no longer needed, for the vessel that had called for assistance had not been heard of since.

The crew of the St. Ives life-boat were experienced men, with medals and many years' service to their credit—all except one man. That one man had never been on a life-boat service before. His name was William Freeman—the only survivor! He had insisted on taking the place of one of the regular crew who was preparing to go out although he was ill. Coxswain Thomas Cocking had spent most of his sixty-five years in the service and had held the post since 1928. Since the station at St. Ives was opened in 1840 it had saved 434 lives and never lost one of its crew. On this grim night it had not seen the wreck nor saved a single man, and lost seven of its members. But this should be remembered: on the 129 occasions its boats had gone to aid vessels in distress the danger of disaster had been there and had been accepted by the life-boatmen as part of their job.

THE LOSS OF THE MUMBLES CREW

The details of the catastrophe that overtook the Mumbles life-boat on 23rd April 1947 will never be known for no man lived to tell what happened—the story had to be pieced together from the evidence of the wreckage.

Mumbles has been a life-boat station since 1835. It is on the west side of Swansea Bay in South Wales, and the spot where the life-boat was wrecked lies on the other side of the bay at Sker Point.

The honorary secretary of the life-boat station had received a message that the 7,000 ton steamship *Samtampa* was drifting towards Nash Shoal. In view of her danger the motor life-boat *Edward Prince of Wales* was launched.

A south-west gale was making the sea rough at the Mumbles but across the bay conditions were much worse; a wind of sixty-five miles per hour was lashing the sea there to a frenzy.

At 6 p.m., when the life-boat had just got away, the coastguard received a message from the *Samtampa*: "Have both hooks down and hope to keep off shoal, but doubtful."

The ship was then west of Porthcawl. The lifeboat returned in answer to the coastguard's signal and was given the latest position of the steamship. She got away again at about 7 p.m. Across the bay the anchors of the *Samtampa* had not saved her and the hurricane-force wind had blown her not on to Nash Shoal but Sker Point.

In an hour great waves broke the ship into three parts. The sea was strewn with wreckage and coated with thick, black oil from the burst fuel tanks. A rocket life-saving apparatus tried to get a rope to the wreck where men had been seen moving about, but the wind was too strong and the lines were blown back. They could do no more, and had to wait for hours until the tide dropped, which was at two o'clock next morning. A policeman then crossed the seaweed-covered rocks to the wreck and searched for survivors. No one was found. The *Samtampa*'s whole crew of forty-one had been swept away.

What had been happening during this time on the other side of Swansea Bay? The life-boat had been watched until she disappeared in the mist and fading light three miles out at sea. Nothing more was heard of her and anxiety increased until, at 5 a.m. the Institution was informed and the Deputy Chief Inspector was sent at once to the Mumbles.

At 6 a.m. the tragedy was discovered. The Mumbles life-boat was found, in the dawn, upside down on the rocks at Sker Point, a few hundred yards from the wrecked *Samtampa*. Three of her crew were lying close at hand, the others further along the shore. All were wearing their life-belts.

What had happened to the men of the Mumbles in the darkness of that storm-tossed bay? Officers of the Institution examined the wrecked boat and tried to make the evidence tell the story that no man would ever tell. The facts they established showed almost beyond doubt what had happened. The crew were not novices; they knew the dangers of this bay, where twice before a life-boat had met disaster. Coxswain William Gammon, aged forty-six, was one of the finest coxswains in the service. He had been seventeen years an officer of the life-boat and held the gold and bronze medals. The men under him were all experienced. They crossed the churned bay making for Sker Point and found conditions worse as they progressed. At about ten o'clock, just before the tide reached its peak, as they were nearing the wreck, a mountainous wave reared above them in the darkness and before the coxswain or the crew could do anything about it their fine boat had capsized and they were thrown into the sea. The boat was lifted on to a shelf of rocks which is normally high and dry, but with the gale and flood tide that night it was under water. The upturned boat was pushed over the boulders and left for the seekers to find at day-break.

There was barely a scratch on the paintwork of the red, white and blue hull, but everything above deck had been torn out or sheared off. Across the rocky shelf was a trail of little things: screws, bolts and mahogany splinters. They told where the boat had been pushed by the sea. The engine was in working order, the controls were correctly set at half-speed and the throttle at a little over half-speed. It was therefore clear she was undamaged and under control at the moment when she capsized; all the damage had been done as she was washed upside down over the rocks.

That night Sker Point claimed forty-nine victims—the entire crews of the steamship and the Mumbles life-boat. When the wind dropped to a fresh breeze and the waters lapped the bottom of the rocky shelf, the two wrecks lying there told a grim tale of the dangers faced by the merchant navy and the life-boat service.

The life-boat could not be salvaged, but parts of the engine were removed and then paraffin-soaked brushwood was placed beneath the hull and set alight. The funeral pyre of that fine boat brought lumps to the throats of the watchers.

From all over the world money came in to help the bereaved families. Well over £90,000 was received, a token of the nation-wide sympathy for these splendid men. Inspired by their example other men volunteered to form a new crew, and less than two months after the disaster the new boat arrived. They named her the *William Gammon*!

Five post-war life-boat capsizes have shown the need for re-equipping the fleet with self-righting boats. Among these disasters was the overturning of the *George Elmy*, Seaham Harbour's 35 ft. Liverpool type boat, in November 1962. Under her coxswain John Miller, and four other men, they went to a local coble, the *Economy*, in distress and picked up her crew of four men and a boy. But, in raging seas, as the *George Elmy* entered Seaham port between the piers, she capsized and all aboard perished except 82-year-old Donald Burrell, one of the coble's crew. The nation was stunned by the tragedy—the worst sea disaster since the port was built in 1828.

More recently, on the wild night of 17th March 1969, the Longhope life-boat *TGB*, a 57 ft. non-self-righter with a crew of eight, went to help the *Irene*, but near the Skerries a mountainous freak wave hit and threw her over. There were no survivors. Ironically, the casualty they had died to help was flung ashore, but her crew of seventeen were swung to the cliff-top and safety by breeches buoy. The moving wall of water which hit the *TGB* was estimated by another life-boat, the 70 ft. *Grace Paterson Ritchie* of Kirkwall, answering the same call, to be 100 ft. high.

Coxswain Daniel Kirkpatrick and two sons, Bob Johnstone and two sons and Eric McFadyen lie in Osmandwall churchyard, but the body of James Swanson was never found. A life-boatman more than anyone else knows the sea is as untamed as ever.

9 The Service in War and Peace

Life-boat work is hazardous enough in peacetime but when war comes the dangers are doubled. In the First World War the youngest and strongest of the crews were taken by the Forces, leaving middle-aged and old men to man the boats, and boat building was practically stopped, yet the number of calls for help increased. Nearly all life-boats were the pulling and sailing type (even by the end of the war there were only nineteen motor life-boats), and it was back- and heart-breaking work for the elderly crews. Yet, in spite of everything, 4,131 lives were saved in the four war years, and some glorious pages of life-boat history written. The difficulties and perils, however, were not easily forgotten.

When the Second World War came the life-boatmen did not think things could be any worse—but they were soon undeceived. Changes came thick and fast. A third of the Institution's administrative staff were taken for the Armed Services. At one time the life-boats could not launch without permission from the naval duty officer. The Navy took control of lights, beacons and all shipping movements around the coast. The lights of most lighthouses, lightships and buoys were extinguished. The coastline was plunged into darkness and ships had to grope their way over the waters with no lights on deck except the compass light. The black-out was strictly enforced and the life-boats had to comply like all shipping. The use of flares for signalling was forbidden. Crews had to hurry in total darkness to the boathouse over beaches bristling with barbed wire and obstacles of coastal defence. A small light was permitted in the boathouse but there were no floodlights or acetylene flares, and launchings had to be made in darkness. In an emergency a life-boat was allowed to ask for harbour lights to be put on for a few minutes, and the aid of searchlights was sometimes given, but nearly all the work of life-saving was done in darkness. The perils of finding a way at night through the shallow waters of the coast with unmarked, shifting channels can be imagined. Even coxswains like Henry Blogg, who knew their own coast from a lifetime of experience, would anchor and endure the rigours of a five-hour wait in the Cockle Gat rather than risk pushing on among the treacherous, inky shallows.

Crews could not be summoned by maroon and each member had to be called separately by messenger. Wireless transmission was at first completely banned, but this rule was relaxed later in the war. Listening was, of course, permitted.

The enemy made life very uncertain in the early months of the war by sowing magnetic mines in shipping lanes and harbour entrances. A terrible toll of vessels and lives was taken. Over three hundred ships were lost in the first seven months. No wonder the life-boats were busy! In the Institution's history those winter months were the busiest and most danger-filled. More lives were saved in each of those four months than in a year of peace.

When the answer to the magnetic mine was found, the enemy used acoustic mines which were detonated by the vibration of a ship's engines or the rattle of the anchor chain.

To the ever-present danger of mines was added the likelihood of enemy aircraft swooping out of the sky to machine-gun or bomb small craft. Lightships and even life-boats were not respected by some Nazi airmen, and although no life-boat was lost in this way, several crews had most uncomfortable experiences.

The first life-boat rescue came just a week after the outbreak of war. The Aldeburgh boat saved seventy-four men from a steamer that had struck a mine and broken in halves. The survivors, wounded and stunned by the explosion, were covered in thick oil. They were taken to hospital or shelter while the life-boatmen set to work to clean up their boat. It took well over two hours to remove the blood and oil. The work of the life-boats in the Second World War had begun in grim earnest!

As if the dangers of attacks by a merciless enemy and of navigating in total darkness were not enough, the winter of 1939 was unusually severe—in fact, at some places, it was the worst in living memory. The heavily increased work had to be done under semi-arctic conditions. One boat was frozen in the ice of the River Ouse and all the crew suffered from frost-bite. Other boats returned with a thick crust of ice on everything including the oilskins and sou'westers of the crews. On some nights the spray froze as it fell.

Moreover, at low tide steel spikes were driven into the beaches to be covered by the sea. They were anti-invasion obstacles designed to rip the bottom out of enemy boats coming ashore. They made a terrible hazard for any life-boat attempting to help a ship driven on to a beach. Land mines were sown by our own soldiers on beaches near the boat-houses and the sea often shifted them in an alarming way. And, of course, beaches were blocked by barbed-wire barriers with a small gap left for the life-boat. This gap sometimes had to be negotiated in the dark. In one instance a boat carriage was guided through the barrier by the glow of cigarette ends. So a life-boatman's job in wartime is anything but dull.

When the British Expeditionary Force was hurriedly

evacuated from Dunkirk the Institution received an urgent summons to send as many life-boats as it could to Dover. The telephone wires hummed and eighteen stations around the 190 miles of coast between Shoreham and Gorleston were told to assemble their boats at Dover. The Ramsgate and Margate boats got off for France at once, straight from their stations on their fifty-mile trip. Their crews were fitted with steel helmets, gas masks and cans of fresh water for the soldiers. The Ramsgate boat towed eight wherries across the Channel for use in the shallow water off the shore and they proved invaluable. During the first night eight hundred men were carried from the chaos of the bombed beaches to ships waiting in deep water, and in three days' magnificent effort 2,800 soldiers were helped to safety. Then, battered and scarred, with her crew utterly exhausted, the life-boat returned home.

The Margate boat took six hundred men off the beaches.

One unnamed life-boat, straight from the builders' yard, also went to France, to bring the total up to nineteen taking part in the evacuation. Just how many men were moved by them is not known, for all were taken over by naval crews except the Ramsgate and Margate boats. But every boat helped in the "miracle of Dunkirk". Mechanics of other life-boats did excellent work at Dover, swiftly repairing damaged small craft that put into the harbour during the evacuation thus enabling them to go back and continue the work.

In peacetime, fishing boats make the highest number of calls on the life-boats; in the last war, aircraft headed the list. This was particularly so on the East Coast. The Navy and the Air Force had their own Air-Sea Rescue Services. But although their boats could rip through the water at forty knots they were not fit for heavy weather and the life-boats supplemented their work. During the Battle of Britain, life-boat stations were warned to stand by when an air battle seemed imminent, and during that vital struggle for the mastery of the Channel sky the life-boats went out a hundred times to answer "MAY-

DAY" reports—the international distress call—and saved eighteen airmen.

One of the men picked up by the Margate boat was a young pilot of a Spitfire squadron. He was temporarily blinded and badly burned; experiences which he described in his well-known book, *The Last Enemy*. His name was Pilot Officer Richard Hope Hillary, and he was a descendant of Sir William Hillary, founder of the Institution. Little could Sir William have dreamt that his plans to help humanity would save one of his own family from the sea more than a century later!

In 1940 the life-boats were launched a thousand times—four hundred more than the average yearly number.

Off the coast of Norfolk and Lincolnshire, life-boats were particularly busy with returning Allied bombers. Many, shot through by enemy flak, had almost regained the coast of Britain when their damaged engines or structures gave way and they came down "in the drink". The life-boat coxswains were given warning when the bombers were expected to return and they made arrangements to launch at top speed if required, for time was even more important with aircraft than with ships. Sometimes the crew were taken from their swamped dinghy in a choppy sea. At other times they were found clinging to the wings or even the tail of their plane which was slowly sinking nose first.

Altogether, 142 airmen were saved in 1,050 launchings to aircraft. Those figures show the large number of fruitless searches. Five times out of six, after hours of waiting through the cold night followed by a desperately hurried launch, they would find nothing. The sixth time there would be just a patch of oil or a glove floating on the wide dawn-lit waters—or a man wearing a Mae West!

One surprising thing about war rescues was the way the older members of the service responded to the demands of such rigorous missions. The two outstanding coxswains of the Second World War were Henry Blogg of Cromer and Robert

Cross of the Humber. Both were born in the same month in 1876, and were thus over sixty when war broke out. The strain imposed on them was terrific. They not only stood up to it but stirred the country with their deeds at a time when heroism was almost common currency. The average age of many crews was fifty, and of some even fifty-five. These middle-aged or old men bore the brunt of the hardest and most dangerous services in the Institution's history.

One of the finest stories of the war years was the rescue by the Peterhead life-boat of the crews from three steamers driven into Peterhead Bay. In January 1942 a gale with gusts up to 105 m.p.h. swept the rocky shore with frightening fury. The ships all dropped anchor but found little shelter, for the wind lay full into the bay. The seas were so violent the anchors would not hold and the vessels were driven, one by one, on to the rocks. So furious was the storm that a hundred feet of the three-hundred-foot granite breakwater was torn away. For seventy-four hours the Peterhead crew were either standing by at instant readiness or battling their way to aid the distressed ships, and they had but twelve hours' sleep in that long period. The life-boat was badly battered on the rocks, squalls of snow blinded the crew and the seas were fearsome. But in three services Coxswain John McLean and his men saved 106 lives from the three ships. Two seamen lost their lives in making a wild attempt to reach the shore. The Institution awarded the coxswain the gold medal for his "conspicuous gallantry".

When the war ended the life-boats had been launched 3,760 times and had saved 6,373 lives, not including the men who had been taken off the beaches at Dunkirk. There were over 1,300 foreign seamen in that number.

What was the cost? Considering the terrible man-made and natural dangers it was smaller than could have been hoped: thirteen life-boatmen had laid down their lives to rescue over six thousand persons; one boat was left on the Dunkirk beaches; three were destroyed in the Cowes building yard by air attack, and two were captured in the Channel Islands; the Tynemouth and Ramsgate stations were closed for a time by enemy bombing, and over a score of other stations were damaged. It could have been much, much worse. The work of the service was hampered—but never stopped.

So the six years of war ended, and the abnormal dangers of that fearful time ended too. But the life-boat service did not disband; the work went on, for the need was still there. Storms, collisions, fires, accidents and stranding still imperilled life at sea. The lag in boat building caused by the war years was slowly made good. Improvements continued, and the efficiency of the boats steadily increased. Public support has been maintained and in 1953 the Institution received the largest legacy in its history—£130,000 from Mrs. E. M. Gordon Cubbin.

There are now 134 conventional life-boat stations, 116 inshore life-boat stations in summer and 37 in winter. Up to 31st May 1973, 97,037 lives had been saved since the Institution was founded. Her Majesty Queen Elizabeth II is Patron and His Royal Highness the Duke of Kent is President.

The fitting of radar in ships has been a great aid to navigation. For years it was not successful in life-boats owing to their lack of height in the water, but in 1963 it was successfully fitted and used at Yarmouth in the Isle of Wight. Direction-finding equipment is an inestimable boon to ships and life-boats. It enables the latter to steer a direct course in darkness or mist to a vessel in trouble. Some larger life-boats have an automatic pilot also and a Decca navigator to assist navigation.

Today all conventional and inshore life-boats have very high frequency (VHF) radio-telephony enabling the crew to communicate with ship, shore and also helicopter. Sea craft and aircraft are thus linked in the work of life-saving.

A typical example of this kind of co-operation took place early in the morning of New Year's Day 1959. The Humber life-boat was investigating red flares which had been seen several miles out to sea off the Yorkshire coast. The waves were high and the life-boat was handicapped by restricted visibility, but a helicopter which had joined in the search spotted two men in a boat off Withernsea. Immediately a message was passed to the Humber crew directing them to the spot. The two men were rescued by the life-boat.

The helicopter has great advantages over the life-boat because of its speed and ability to reach a casualty on rocks or sand banks where nothing afloat can get to it. Moreover, exhausted or injured men can be taken direct to hospital with no delay. This was dramatically demonstrated in February 1956, when two naval and a R.A.F. helicopter took forty-one men from the Norwegian freighter *Dovrefjell*, which had run on to a shelf of rocks in the Pentland Skerries. The Longhope and Wick life-boats immediately went to the vessel's aid, but the high, confused seas breaking over the wreck prevented the boats going alongside. The helicopters arrived and took it in turns to fly over the bridge, pick up a seaman and get clear of the vessel while hauling him into the helicopter by winch. All were saved.

But the helicopter cannot work in darkness or fog or in a very strong wind. Nor can it tow a ship to safety or help with salvage work, although experiments are now being undertaken in this respect.

So both life-boat and helicopter have their limitations, but their advantages can be pooled when necessary as happened in September 1959 when there were two fine instances of teamwork in joint air and sea operations. One was at Shoreham Harbour, Sussex, and the other in the Isle of Wight. In both cases the helicopters were first to reach the sailing boats in distress and they took off the endangered crews and the life-boats towed the boats to safety.

The use of helicopters was in fact seriously considered by the Institution as far back as 1948 when trials were undertaken. In 1955, following advances in performance and design, a special sub-committee examined the possibilities of using helicopters in conjunction with life-boats. Their recommendation was that the Institution should not build its own helicopters but develop co-operation with the Royal Navy and Royal Air Force and also with the U.S. Air Force, all of which operate helicopters in their own Air-Sea Rescue Services and cover most of our coastline in this way. The R.N.L.I. has done this, and now the honorary secretary of a branch can ask, through the coastguard, for helicopter aid if he needs it.

This is an age of plastics, and use of this versatile material has been brought into life-boat construction, particularly with the production of the 18 ft. G.R.P. (glass reinforced plastic) boat designed by Mr. J. A. McLachlan and bearing his name. The rigid hull has ragged chines (ridges), which reduce the flat surface exposed to the sea when at top speed of twenty-two knots. First ordered in 1969, seven boats have been built and have proved successful. Two 49 h.p. diesel engines power the craft.

Although one delegate at a life-boat conference, with a doubt about new materials, wittily remarked, "Before you go in for plastics touch wood," the R.N.L.I. believes that any new equipment or material science produces should be studied, tested, even if not applied to life-saving.

The Institution has thus kept pace with modern developments and changing methods. It is ready to try anything that will help in the job of saving life from shipwreck. It encourages rescue efforts from the shore, giving medals where fishing boats put out or swimmers strive to rescue those in danger. The Institution does not say, "We can only give our blessing if you use a life-boat." The aim is to save life.

It is true that radio, radar, accurate broadcast weather reports and gale warnings have made the seas safer than ever before for shipping, but the need for a life-boat service remains. The number of launches increases each year. In the 'fifties it was over 700, but in June, July and August 1972 there were

1,064 launches. This great rise is largely due to summer calls on Inshore Rescue craft. In fact, life-boats are busier now than in any peace years during the 150 years history of the Service. The words of Sir William Hillary's Appeal still apply:

"So long as man shall continue to navigate the ocean, and the tempests shall hold their course over its surface, in every age and on every coast, disasters by sea, shipwreck and peril to human life must inevitably take place."

And when disaster does overtake the seaman the sight of the red, blue and white boat cleaving the seas as she hastens towards him brings new hope. The cry goes up: "The life-boat is coming", and numbed limbs find new strength, despair is thrown off, the shipwrecked mariner knows—the whole world knows—that in spite of all other changes the magnificent, self-sacrificing spirit of the life-boat service has not changed.

Appendices

The Appendices are reproduced by kind permission of the R.N.L.I. from Oliver Warner's The Life-boat Service

Appendix I

GOLD MEDAL AWARDS

The list of Gold Medals awarded by the R.N.L.I. includes "Second Service Clasps" where indicated. Ranks are given as at the time of the service concerned. S.C. = Service Clasp.

Name and Rank where appropriate	*Station where appropriate*	*Casualty where appropriate*	*Date of Award*
H.M. King George IV		Honorary	14 May 1825
H.R.H. The Duke of York		Honorary	14 May 1825
His Grace the Archbishop of Canterbury		Honorary	14 May 1825
Fremantle, C. H. Captain, R.N.	Christchurch	Unknown Swedish Brig	10 July 1824
Clarke, Joseph Lieutenant, R.N.	Birling (Eastbourne)	Brig *Juno*	8 Dec. 1824
Hillary, Sir William Baronet		Awarded as Founder. (Sir William Hillary's later awards were bestowed for gallantry)	10 March 1825
Manby, G. W. Captain		Presented as a testimony of the great utility of his life-saving apparatus	10 March 1825
Bennett, C. G. Captain, R.N.	Lyme Regis	Ship *Unity*	5 Jan. 1825
Grandy, S. Lieutenant, R.N.	Portsmouth	Ship *Admiral Berkeley*	9 Feb. 1825
Randall, Henry Lieutenant, R.N., Coastguard	Elie N.B.	Ship *Devoran*	9 Feb. 1825
Peake, Thomas L. Captain, R.N.		Ship *Admiral Berkeley*	2 March 1825
De St Croix, Mr P.	St Helier	*Fanny* of St Malo	27 July 1825
De St Croix, Mr Francis	St Helier	*Fanny* of St Malo	27 July 1825
De St Croix, Mr Jean	St Helier	*Fanny* of St Malo	27 July 1825
Morris, John Rowe Captain, R.N., Coastguard	Newcastle, Ireland	Ship *Richard Pope*	5 April 1826

Name and Rank where appropriate	*Station where appropriate*	*Casualty where appropriate*	*Date of Award*
Wilson, Thomas Member of Parliament		Chairman—1824–52	18 April 1826
Joy, McGeorge Master, H.M. Cutter *Mermaid*	Holy Island	Ship *John & Jessie*	13 Sept. 1826
Else, Lieutenant, R.N.	Fowey	Ship *Providence*	18 Oct. 1826
Bowen, C. H. Lieutenant, R.N.	Fraserburgh	*Rose* of Wick	31 Jan. 1827
Lindsay, James Lieutenant, R.N.	Fort George	Sloop *Lively*	7 Feb. 1827
Jobson, Christopher Lieutenant, R.N., Coastguard	Arbroath	Ship *Alice*	28 March 1827
Matthews, R. B. Lieutenant, R.N.	Lowestoft	*The Lord Duncan*	24 Oct. 1827
Hillary, Sir William (2nd S.C.) Baronet	Isle of Man	Ship *Fortroendert*	16 Jan. 1828
Blois, J. R. Captain, R.N.	Glynn, Ireland	Steamer *Venus*	20 Aug. 1828
Brunden, J. Lieutenant, R.N. Chief Officer of Coastguard	Boulmer	Schooner *Triton*	10 Dec. 1828
Lloyd, Sam Lieutenant, R.N., Coastguard	Ballycotton	Brig *Capricho* (Spanish)	18 Feb. 1829
Broad, William Lloyd's Agent	Falmouth	Brig *Sarah*	10 June 1829
Lingard, John Lieutenant, R.N.	Whitby	Brig *Esther*	19 Aug. 1829
Hutchison, H. Lieutenant, R.N.	Kingshorn	Brig *Duke*	11 Nov. 1829
Graham, Philip Captain, R.N.	Walmer	Brig *Mountaineer*	10 Feb. 1830
Johnson, W. W. P. Lieutenant, R.N.	Walmer	Brig *Mountaineer*	10 Feb. 1830
Walls, Wm. Stephen Lieutenant, R.N.	Walmer	Brig *Mountaineer*	10 Feb. 1830
Jones, Richard Lieutenant, R.N., Coastguard	Whitby	Brig *Smalls*	10 Feb. 1830
Prattent, John Lieutenant, R.N.	Hastings, H.M. *Hyperion*	Lugger *La Constance* (French)	10 March 1830

Name and Rank where appropriate	*Station where appropriate*	*Casualty where appropriate*	*Date of Award*
James, Horatio Lieutenant, R.N.	Hastings, H.M. *Hyperion*	Lugger *La Constance* (French)	10 March 1830
Hillary, Sir William (3rd S.C.) Baronet	Isle of Man	Sloop *Eclipse*	27 Nov. 1830
Hillary, Sir William (4th S.C.) Baronet	Isle of Man	Steamer *St George*	15 Dec. 1830
Robinson, Robert Lieutenant, R.N.	Isle of Man	Steamer *St George*	15 Dec. 1830
Manby, G. W. Captain (2nd S.C.)		For his method for forcing boats from a beach through a heavy surf	15 Dec. 1830
Jones, Richard (2nd S.C.) Lieutenant, R.N., Coastguard		Sloop *Northfield*	5 Jan. 1831
James, William Lieutenant, R.N.	Falmouth	Brig *Le Bon Père*	5 Jan. 1831
H.M. King William IV		As Patron	30 March 1831
Earle, E. C. Lieutenant, R.N.	Rye	Brig *Fame*	4 May 1831
Steane, John Lieutenant, R.N.	Rye	Brig *Fame*	4 May 1831
Turner, Charles Lieutenant, R.N.	Fraserburgh	Sloop *Janet*	1 June 1831
Leigh, Thomas Lieutenant, R.N., Coastguard	Winterton	Brig *Annabella Colm*	21 Sept 1831
Parey, R. M. Lieutenant, R.N.	Rye	Fishing boat *L'Arnée*	25 Jan. 1832
Leigh, Thomas (2nd S.C.) Lieutenant, R.N., Coastguard	Winterton	Ship *Crawford Davison*	24 April 1833
Sumner, W. Richard Surgeon	Formby, Liverpool	Pilot Boat *Good Intent*	12 Dec. 1833
Snell, George Lieutenant, R.N., Coastguard	Dungeness	Brig *Pioneer*	29 Jan. 1834
Randall, Henry (2nd S.C.) Lieutenant, R.N., Coastguard	Anstruther	Schooner *Wanderer*	21 May 1834

Name and Rank where appropriate	*Station where appropriate*	*Casualty where appropriate*	*Date of Award*
Owen, William Master Mariner	Holyhead	Ship *Plutarch* (American)	7 Oct. 1835
Williams, Rev. James	Holyhead	*Active Sarah*	7 Oct. 1835
Somerville, John Lieutenant, R.N., Coastguard	New Romney	Brig *Industry*	28 Oct. 1835
Cox, H. Lieutenant, R.N., Chief Officer, Coastguard	St Andrews	Schooner *Tid* of Dundee	28 Oct. 1835
Jelland, W. John Master Mariner	*The Agendria* (at sea)	*Francis Speight*	10 March 1836
Walsh, W. Martin Master Mariner	Wexford	Ship *Glasgow* (American)	16 Aug. 1837
Essell, William Folkes Lieutenant, R.N., Coastguard	Carnsore	Sloop *Anne and Elizabeth*	28 Feb. 1838
Stark, Peter Lieutenant, R.N., Coastguard	Broughty Ferry	*Ranger of Perth*	21 March 1838
Rymer, D. Lieutenant, R.N., Chief Officer Coastguard	Berwick	Schooner *Margaret of Dundee*	9 May 1838
Hoed, W. Francis Philip Master Mariner	Netherlands Ship *Phénomene*	Ship *Columbia* of Liverpool	6 June 1838
Browne, P. R., Captain	Dundrum	Schooner *Bloom*	15 Nov. 1838
Britain, G. S. Lieutenant, R.N.	Whitby	Brig *Jupiter* of Whitby	15 Nov. 1838
Ross, Thomas Captain, R.N., Inspecting Commander Coastguard	Swords District, Ireland	Brig *Gainsborough*	9 Jan. 1839
Symmes, H. A. S. Lieutenant, R.N.	Isle of Wight	Brig *Claire* (French)	9 Jan. 1839
Lett, S. J. Lieutenant, R.N., Chief Officer of Coastguard	Rosslare, Ireland	Ship *Ariadne*	9 Jan. 1839
Thompson, R. K. Chief Officer, Coastguard	Clogher Head	Schooner *Minerva*	17 April 1839

Name and Rank where appropriate	*Station where appropriate*	*Casualty where appropriate*	*Date of Award*
Collins, John Master Mariner	American ship *Roscius*	Ship *Scotia*	8 Jan. 1840
Metherall, R. R. Lieutenant, R.N., Coastguard	Youghal	Brig *Medora*	15 April 1840
Sewell, H. J. Lieutenant, R.N., Coastguard	Newcastle (Co. Down)	Smack *Sarah*	9 Nov. 1840
Marsh, Digby Captain, R.N., Coastguard	Brighton	Brig *Mary*, Schooner *Sir John Seale*, Brig *Offerton*	17 Dec. 1840
Macnamara, Timothy Lieutenant, R.N., Coastguard	Littlehampton	*Billy Boy Victoria.* Sloop *Lively*	17 Dec. 1840
Steel, W. Charles Coastguard	Scilly	Steamer *Thames*	4 March 1841
Quadling, W. B. E. Chief Officer, Coastguard	Courtmacsherry (Co. Cork)	Brig *Salona*	13 April 1842
Vicary, William Lieutenant, R.N., Coastguard	Atherfield, Isle of Wight	Brig *George*	8 Feb. 1843
Bulley, John Lieutenant, R.N., Coastguard	Atherfield, Isle of Wight	Brig *George*	8 Feb. 1843
Britton, John Master Mariner	At sea. American ship *Rochester*	Ship *Dorchester*	30 July 1845
Bulley, John (2nd S.C.) Lieutenant, R.N., Coastguard	Atherfield, Isle of Wight	Ship *Llanrumney*	10 Feb. 1848
Pym, R. E. Lieutenant, R.N.	Whitby	Fishing boat *Harm* of Christchurch	5 Nov. 1848
Goss, Thomas Lieutenant, R.N., Coastguard	Dunmanus	Ship *Mountaineer*	16 Jan. 1851
Davies, George Captain, R.N.	Penzance	Brig *New Commercial* of Whitby	30 Jan. 1851
Howard, T. R. Commander	Penzance	Brig *New Commercial* of Whitby	30 Jan. 1851
Palmer, George Member of Parliament	Nazing Park, Essex	In consideration of the services of the life-boats built on his plan	3 March 1853

Name and Rank where appropriate	*Station where appropriate*	*Casualty where appropriate*	*Date of Award*
Ludlow, Isaac Captain	At sea. American ship *Monmouth* of New York	Ship *Meuadan*	5 Jan. 1854
Hamilton, H. A. Chief boatman, Coastguard	Balbriggan	Brig *Tregiste* of Trieste	2 Dec. 1858
Peake, James H.M. Dockyard	Devonport	Designer of the life-boat of the Institution	3 Feb. 1859
Rodgers, Joseph Seaman *Royal Charter*	Anglesey	Steamer *Royal Charter* of Liverpool	3 Nov. 1859
Cobb, Rev. Charles	Dymchurch	Lugger *Courrier de Dieppe* of Dieppe	17 Jan. 1867
Perrott, Sir Edward G. L. Baronet		Presented for his long and most valuable services as Chairman of the Preparatory Committee of the Institution	7 March 1872
Elyard, Captain Honorary Secretary at Broadstairs Branch	Broadstairs	Schooner *Lion* of Goole	6 April 1876
Cubitt, Wm. Son of Hon. Sec.	Bacton	Schooner *Richard Warbrick* of Fleet-wood	5 Feb. 1880
Torrens, John Lieutenant, 2nd Dragoons	Poolbeg	Schooner *Robert Brown* of Waven-point	6 Jan. 1881
Fish, Chas. E. Coxswain	Ramsgate	Ship *Indian Chief* of Liverpool	25 Jan. 1881
Chapman, Thomas Chairman, F.R.S.		Chairman, 1873–83	5 April 1883
Ward, Vice-Admiral John Ross Chief Inspector of Life-boats		Served the Institution 1852–83	7 June 1883
Fish, Charles E. (2nd S.C.) Coxswain	Ramsgate	On his retirement	8 Oct. 1891
McCombie, Thos. Master of Irish lights	Dublin	Ship *Palme* of Finland	9 Jan. 1896

Name and Rank where appropriate	*Station where appropriate*	*Casualty where appropriate*	*Date of Award*
Haylett, James Late Assistant Coxswain	Caister	Services during 50 years, and at accident to No. 2 Lifeboat	9 Feb. 1905
Rees, Daniel Solicitor	Barry	Yacht *Firefly*	11 July 1907
Owen, Milliani Coxswain	Holyhead	S.S. *Harold* of Liverpool	12 March 1908
O'Shea, Rev. John Michael	Ardmore	Schooner *Teaser* of Montrose	13 April 1911
Langlands, Thomas Coxswain	Whitby	S.S. *Rohilla*	12 Nov. 1914
Smith, Robert Coxswain	Tynemouth	S.S. *Rohilla*	12 Nov. 1914
Burton, Captain H. E. Hon. Superintendent of Motor-boat	Tynemouth	S.S. *Rohilla*	12 Nov. 1914
Blogg, Henry George Coxswain	Cromer	S.S. *Fernebo*	9 Feb. 1917
Howells, John Coxswain	Fishguard	Schooner *Hermina* of Rotterdam	17 Dec. 1920
Swan, John J. Coxswain	Lowestoft	S.S. *Hopelyn* of Newcastle	17 Nov. 1922
Fleming, Wm. G. Coxswain	Gorleston	S.S. *Hopelyn* of Newcastle	17 Nov. 1922
North and South Holland Lifeboat Society		Centenary of that Society	18 Nov. 1924
South Holland Life-saving Society		Centenary of that Society	18 Nov. 1924
Jones, Captain Owen Volunteer Life-boatman	Moelfre	Ketch *Excel* of Poole	17 Nov. 1927
Roberts, William Second Coxswain	Moelfre	Ketch *Excel* of Poole	17 Nov. 1927
Blogg, Henry George (2nd S.C.) Coxswain	Cromer	Dutch oil tanker *Georgia*	15 Dec. 1927
Patton, Robert Coxswain	Runswick	S.S. *Dispenser* of West Hartlepool	8 March 1934
Sliney, Patrick Coxswain	Ballycotton	Daunt Rock Lightship	12 March 1936
Cross, Robert Coxswain	Humber	S.T. *Gurth* of Grimsby	14 March 1940
Boyle, John Coxswain	Arranmore	S.S. *Stolwyke* of Rotterdam	17 April 1941

Name and Rank where appropriate	*Station where appropriate*	*Casualty where appropriate*	*Date of Award*
Blogg, Henry George (3rd S.C.) Coxswain	Cromer No. 1	S.S. *Oxshott*, S.S. *Gallois*, S.S. *Deerwood* and S.S. *Paddy Hendly*	11 Sept. 1941
McLean, John B. Coxswain	Peterhead	S.S. *Runswick*, S.S. *Fiora* and S.S. *Saltwick*	12 March 1942
Bennison, Lieut. W. H. Coxswain	Hartlepool	S.S. *Hawkwood* of London	12 March 1942
Murphy, Patrick Coxswain	Newcastle (Co. Down)	S.S. *Browning* of Liverpool	21 May 1942
Cross, Robert (2nd S.C.) Coxswain	Humber	H.M.T. *Almondine*	11 Feb. 1943
Gammon, William J. Coxswain	The Mumbles	H.M.C.S. *Cheboque*	14 Dec. 1944
King, Thomas J. Coxswain	St Helier, Jersey	Yacht *Maurice Georges* of Jersey	8 Dec. 1949
Evans, Richard M. Coxswain	Moelfre	M.V. *Hindlea*	10 Dec. 1959
Petit, Capt. Hubert Ernest Coxswain	St Peter Port	Norwegian M.V. *Johan Collett*	11 April 1963
German Life-boat Society	Bremen	On the occasion of the Centenary in 1965	10 Dec. 1964
French Central Life-boat Society	Paris	On the occasion of the Centenary in 1965	10 Dec. 1964
Harvey, Lieut-Cdr. Harold Inspector of Life-boats	Holyhead	Greek M.V. *Nafsiporos*	12 Jan. 1967
Evans, Richard M. Coxswain	Moelfre	Greek M.V. *Nafsiporos*	12 Jan. 1967
Marina, Princess H.R.H. Duchess of Kent		To mark the 25th Anniversary of her appointment as President	12 Jan. 1967
H.M. Coastguard		To mark the 150th Anniversary of foundation of Coastguard in 1822	9 Feb. 1972

Appendix II

PRINCIPAL OFFICERS

1 Patrons

Successive Sovereigns have been Patrons of the Institution since King George IV in 1824.

2 Presidents

The Earl of Liverpool, 1824–8
The Fourth Duke of Northumberland, 1851–65
The Sixth Duke of Northumberland, 1866–99
H.R.H. Albert Edward, Prince of Wales (King Edward VII), 1900–1
H.R.H. the Duke of York and Cornwall, afterwards Prince of Wales (King George V), 1902–10
The Seventh Duke of Northumberland, 1911–18
H.R.H. Edward, Prince of Wales (King Edward VIII), 1919–36
H.R.H. Albert, Duke of York (King George VI), 1936
H.R.H. the Duke or Kent, 1936–42
H.R.H. Princess Marina, Duchess of Kent, 1943–68
H.R.H. The Duke of Kent, 1969–

3 Chairmen of the Committee of Management

Thomas Wilson, M.P., 1824–52
Alderman William Thompson, M.P., 1852–3
Thomas Baring, M.P., F.R.S., 1854–73
Thomas Chapman, F.R.S., 1873–83
Sir Edward Birkbeck, Bart., M.P., 1883–1908
Colonel Sir Fitzroy Clayton, K.C.V.O., 1908–1911
Earl Waldegrave, P.C., 1911–23
Sir Godfrey Baring, Bart., K.B.E., 1923–56
Commodore the Earl Howe, P.C., C.B.E., 1956–64
Captain the Hon. V. M. Wyndham-Quin, R.N., 1964–8
Admiral Sir Wilfrid Woods, C.B.E., K.C.B., D.S.O., 1968–72
Commander F. R. H. Swann, O.B.E., R.N.V.R., 1972–

4 Secretaries

(at the head of the full-time administrative staff)

Thomas Edwards, 1824–50
Richard Lewis, 1850–83
Charles Dibdin, 1883–1910
Sir George Shee, 1910–31
Lieutenant-Colonel C. R. Satterthwaite, 1931–47
Colonel A. D. Burnett Brown, 1947–60
Lieutenant-Colonel Charles Earle, 1960–1

Stirling Whorlow, 1961–9
Captain Nigel Dixon, R.N., 1970–
(From 1970 the title became 'Director and Secretary')

5 Chief Inspectors of Life-boats

(at the head of technical and operational staff)
Commander (later Vice-Admiral) J. Ross Ward, 1852–83
Captain the Hon. H. W. Chetwynd, R.N., 1883–93
Commander St Vincent Nepean, R.N., 1893–1909
Commander Thomas Holmes, R.N., 1909–19
Captain H. F. J. Rowley, R.N., 1919–30
Commander E. D. Drury, R.N., 1930–8
Lieutenant-Commander P. E. Vaux, R.N., 1939–51
Commander T. G. Michelmore, R.N.R., 1951–8
Commander S. W. F. Bennetts, R.N., 1958–61
Lieutenant-Commander W. L. G. Dutton, R.N.R., 1961–

6 Life Vice-Presidents

Air Vice-Marshal Sir Geoffrey R. Bromet, K.B.E., C.B., D.S.O., D.L.
C. G. Freke, Esq., C.I.E.
Sir Arnet Robinson

7 Honorary Life Governors

This is the highest honour which the Institution can confer on honorary workers. It was instituted in 1922, to be conferred only in recognition of long and very distinguished services, and to be accompanied by the presentation of a vellum signed by the President of the Institution.

Living holders of the honour	*Appointed*
The Lady Dorothy D'Oyly Carte	January 1934
Mrs R. H. Edmondson, B.A.	January 1946
Miss Pattie Price	June 1948
Mrs Dorothy Abel Smith, O.B.E.	December 1949
Mrs Miles Thornewill	October 1953
Mrs Graham Goodson	November 1954
John S. Duncan, M.B.E., J.P.	January 1958
Mrs R. M. Lloyd	January 1961
Mrs D. J. Wilkes	January 1964
Lieutenant-Commander H. Th. de Booy	February 1964
B. V. Howell, M.B.E.	January 1965
R. H. Mahony, Esq.	January 1967
Captain G. B. Piggott, D.L., J.P.	January 1967
S. Valentine, M.B.E., B.L.	January 1967
Sir Philip Hay, K.C.V.O., T.D.	January 1967
Air Marshal Sir Brian Baker, K.B.E., C.B., D.S.O., M.C., A.F.C.	January 1971
Alderman Miss Mary Conway Burton	January 1972

Mrs Constance Noyce	January 1972
Captain H. Hansson	May 1972
David Chapel, M.B.E., T.D.	May 1973
Mrs Graham Doggart	May 1973
Prof. William Flexner, Ph.D.	May 1973

8 Vice-Presidents

The Duke of Atholl
Sir Charles C. Baring, Bart., D.L., J.P.
The Archbishop of Canterbury, P.C.
The Marquis Camden, D.L., J.P.
L. C. H. Cave, Esq.
P. Denham Christie, Esq., B.Sc.
Raymond Cory, Esq.
Major-General Ralph H. Farrant, C.B.
Brigadier J. W. H. Gow, C.B.E., D.L., J.P.
Admiral Sir Angus Cunninghame Graham, K.B.E., C.B.
Commander H. G. P. Grenfell, D.S.C., R.N.
Geoffrey Hale, Esq., M.B.E., M.B., B.Ch.
Lieutenant-Commander The Hon. Greville Howard, V.R.D., R.N.R.
Rear-Admiral Sir Edmund Irving, K.B.E., C.B.
Major The Lord Killanin, M.B.E., T.D., M.A., M.R.I.A.
R. Leigh-Wood, Esq., D.L.
The Duke of Northumberland, K.G.
The Duke of Portland, K.G.
Captain R. E. D. Ryder, V.C., R.N.
Commander F. R. H. Swann, O.B.E., R.N.V.R.
N. Warington Smyth, Esq, O.B.E.
Admiral Sir Wilfrid Woods, G.B.E., K.C.B., D.S.O., D.L.
Captain the Hon. V. M. Wyndham-Quin, R.N.

Treasurer: The Duke of Northumberland, K.G.
Deputy Treasurer: D. A. Acland

9 Committee of Management

The President   The Vice-Presidents   The Treasurer
Commander F. R. H. Swann, O.B.E., R.N.V.R., *Chairman*
The Duke of Atholl
Major-General Ralph H. Farrant, C.B. } *Deputy Chairmen*
H.R.H. The Prince Philip, Duke of Edinburgh, K.G.
D. A. Acland, Esq.
Captain Sir George Barnard
Surgeon Captain F. W. Baskerville, C.B.E., L.M.S.S.A., R.N. Rtd.
William T. Bishop, C.B.E., F.R.I.C.S.
A. Burn, Esq.
J. H. B. Chapman, C.B., C.Eng., F.R.N.I.A., R.C.N.C. Rtd.
Philip G. Clarke, Esq.
Philip Colville, Esq., M.B.E.

Vice-Admiral Sir Peter Compston, K.C.B.
W. P. Courtauld, Esq.
Lieut-Colonel R. Crawshaw, O.B.E., T.D., D.L., M.P.
Commander M. Cunningham, Assoc. R.I.N.A., R.N.
Maldwin Drummond, Esq., J.P.
Sir Knowles Edge, Bart., J.P.
Major-General Ralph H. Farrant, C.B.
Marshal of the R.A.F. Sir John Grandy, G.C.B., K.B.E., D.S.O.
Peter Guinness, Esq.
G. Harrison, Esq.
Vice-Admiral Sir Arthur Hezlet, K.B.E., C.B., D.S.O., D.S.C., D.L.
Rear-Admiral D. J. Hoare, C.B., M.I.Mech.E., M.R.I.N.A.
R. G. Hollond, Esq.
Robin Knox-Johnston, Esq., C.B.E.
Frank Lemass, Esq.
W. F. G. Lord, Esq.
Clayton Love, Jnr.
Captain Sir Charles McGregor, Bart.
P. V. MacKinnon, Esq., O.B.E.
Rear-Admiral M. Morgan Giles, D.S.O., O.B.E., G.M., M.P.
Marquis of Normanby, M.B.E.
Peter D. Odlum, Esq.
H. A. W. Oughton, Esq., O.B.E.
Lieutenant-Commander P. E. C. Pickles, M.B.E., J.P., R.N.V.R.
E. G. E. Rayner, Esq.
Air Marshal Sir Anthony Selway, K.C.B., D.F.C.
J. K. Shipton, Esq.
Lieutenant-Commander Jeremy Tetley, R.N. Rtd.
Michael Vernon, Esq.

Ex Officio

The Lord Mayor of London
The Admiral Commanding Reserves and Director-General of Naval Recruiting
The Deputy Master of Trinity House
The Hydrographer of the Navy
The Chairman of Lloyd's
The Master of the Honourable Company of Master Mariners
The Chairman of the Baltic Exchange

10 Administrative and Organizing Staff

Director and Secretary: Captain Nigel Dixon, R.N.
Chief Inspector of Life-boats: Lieutenant-Commander W. L. G. Dutton, O.B.E., R.D., R.N.R.
Deputy Director: J. R. Atterton, M.B.E.
Public Relations Officer: Patrick Howarth
Finance Secretary: J. R. Barnett, F.C.I.S.

Appeals Secretary: V. C. Frank
District Appeals Secretary: Commander E. F. Pritchard, R.N.
Membership Office: G. R. Walton

11 Operational and Technical Staff

Secretary (Operations Division): M. S. Porcher, C.M.G., O.B.E.
Chief Staff Officer (Technical): Symington Macdonald, B.Sc., F.R.I.N.A., M.I.Ess., S.N.A.M.E.
Chief of Operations (Designate): Commander D. B. Cairns, R.D., R.N.R.
Staff Officer Operations: Captain R. M. Dabbs
Staff Officer (Technical): Lieutenant-Commander H. E. Over, C.Eng., M.I.Mech.E., A.M.B.I.M., R.N.
Superintendent of Depot: Lieut.-Commander H. H. Harvey, V.R.D., R.N.R.
Staff Officer Inshore Life-boats (Technical): Lieut. E. D. Stogdon, R.N.V.R.
Resident Engineer (Littlehampton): J. G. Groves

12 Regional Co-ordinators

North: Miss I. E. Morison
West (Designate): Commander P. D. Sturdee, O.B.E., R.N.

13 Regional Inspector of Life-boats

Scotland: Commander P. F. Gladwin, R.D., R.N.R.

14 Inspectors of Life-boats

No. 1 Division (Scottish Region): Flight Lieutenant T. F. Notman, R.A.F.
No. 2 Division (Scottish Region): Lieutenant A. M. Woodroffe, R.N.R.
No. 3 Area: Lieutenant-Commander H. F. Teare, R.D., R.N.R.
No. 4 Area: Lieutenant-Commander R. S. Porchmouth, C.D., R.C.N.
No. 5 Area: Lieutenant-Commander A. W. Tate, R.N.
No. 6 Area: Lieutenant-Commander D. J. Wilford, R.N.R.
No. 7 Area: Lieutenant-Commander G. R. Cooper, R.N.R.
No. 8 Area: Lieutenant-Commander P. F. B. Roe, R.N.
No. 10 Area: Lieutenant-Commander B. Miles, R.N.R.

15 District Organizing Secretaries

Scotland: Miss E. M. Lloyd-Jones
North-East: K. Thirwell
Midlands: Colonel J. T. Benn, O.B.E.
East: G. E. Price
London, North of the Thames: J. R. F. Sims
London, South of the Thames: P. Holness
London, City: H. J. Berry
South-East: I. Wallington
Southern: A. K. Oliver
South-West: A. R. Dickinson
Wales: Miss T. H. Ashe
North-West: Major James G. Disley
Ireland: Lieutenant-Colonel D. H. Clark, M.C., G.M.

Appendix III

PRESENT AND PAST STATIONS OF THE ROYAL NATIONAL LIFE-BOAT INSTITUTION

Hon. Secretaries and Coxswains appear as in the latest (1973) edition of the R.N.L.I. Year Book. Life-boat names are in italics.

An asterisk denotes that there is an Inshore Life-boat, sometimes additional to the regular life-boat.

The closure of stations, as recorded in this list, is always a matter of extreme regret. It is sometimes made inevitable by changing circumstances, such as the fact that, with the increased range of modern life-boats, certain stations can serve a larger area.

Station	*County*	*Date when station was established or taken over by the Institution*	*Date closed*
Aberdeen*	Aberdeen	1802	
Hon. Secs., Captain B. Atkinson and R. M. Addison; Coxswain, Albert Bird (*Ramsay-Dyce*).			
Aberdovey*	Merionethshire	1837	1931 (I.L.B. 1963)
Hon. Sec., Major J. G. Richards, M.B.E.			
Abergele	Denbighshire	1868	1869
Abersoch*	Caernarvonshire	1869	1931 (I.L.B. 1965)
Hon. Sec., David Fletcher-Brewer.			
Aberystwyth*	Cardiganshire	1862	
Hon. Sec., Gwym Martin, D.F.M.			
Ackergill	Caithness	1878	1932
Aith	Shetlands	1933	
Hon. Sec., John D. Garrick, J.P.; Coxswain, Kenneth Henry (*John and Frances Macfarlane*).			
Aldeburgh	Suffolk	1824	
Hon. Sec., D. J. Owen; Coxswain, Reuben Wood (*The Albert and Patience Gottwald*).			
Alderney	Channel Islands	1869	1884
Alnmouth	Northumberland	1853	1935
Amble	Northumberland	1842	
Hon. Sec., John Matthews; Coxswain, John Connell (*Millie Walton*).			
Angle	Pembrokeshire	1867	
Hon. Sec., Major J. N. S. Allen-Minehouse; Coxswain, William Holmes (*Richard Vernon and Mary Garforth of Leeds*).			

Station	*County*	*Date when station was established or taken over by the Institution*	*Date closed*
Anstruther	Fife	1865	
Hon. Sec., Captain W. Anderson; Coxswain James Jack (*The Doctors*).			
Appledore	Devonshire	1825	
Hon. Sec. Ivor Wickersham; Coxswain Desmond Cox (*Louisa Anne Hawker*).			
Arbroath *	Angus	1803	
Hon. Sec., Captain J. Small; Coxswain, Douglas Mathewson (*The Duke of Montrose*).			
Ardmore	Co. Waterford	1858	1895
Ardrossan	Ayr	1869	1930
Arklow	Co. Wicklow	1826	
Hon. Sec., J. Tyrrell; Coxswain, Michael O'Brien (*St Andrew, Civil Service No. 10*).			
Arran Lamlash*	Bute	1970	
Hon. Sec., Captain K. M. Rore.			
Arranmore	Co. Donegal	1883	
Hon. Sec., Bernard Gallagher; Coxswain, Owen Kavanagh (*T.G..B.*).			
Atherfield	Isle of Wight	1890	1915
Atlantic College, St Donat's Castle*	Glamorgan	1963	
Hon. Sec., John L. Lipscombe.			
Ayr	Ayr	1802	1932
Bacton	Norfolk	1857	1882
Balbriggan	Co. Dublin	1875	1898
Balcary	Kirkcudbright	1884	1931
Ballantrae	Ayr	1871	1919
Ballycotton	Co. Cork	1858	
Hon. Sec., D. O'Sullivan; Coxswain, Michael Walsh (*Ethel/Mary*).			
Ballywalter	Co. Down	1866	1906
Baltimore	Co. Cork	1919	
Hon. Sec., Rodger de Quincy; Coxswain, John Collins (*Sarah Tilson*).			
Bamburgh Castle	Northumberland	1786	1898
Banff (*see* **Whitehills**)			
Bangor*	Co. Down	1965	
Hon. Sec., W. E. Hay.			
Barmouth*	Merioneth	1828	
Hon. Sec., Captain T. R. F. Addie; Coxswain, Evan Jones (*The Chieftain*).			
Barmston	Yorkshire	1884	1898

Station	*County*	*Date when station was established or taken over by the Institution*	*Date closed*
Barra Island	Outer Hebrides	1931	

Hon. Sec., Hugh N. Morrison, M.B.E.; Coxswain, John MacLeod (*R. A. Colby Cubbin No. 3*).

Barrow* Lancashire 1864
Hon. Sec., T. Downing; Coxswain, Robert Charnley (*Herbert Leigh*).

Barry Dock Glamorgan 1901
Hon. Sec., Captain J. D. Harries; Coxswain Francis Tinsley (*Arthur and Blanche Harris*).

Beaumaris* Anglesey 1891
Hon. Sec., M. L. Booth; Coxswain William Pritchard (*Field-Marshal and Mrs Smuts*).

Bembridge* Isle of Wight 1867
Hon. Sec., Arthur P. Weaver, B.E.M.; Coxswain, Peter Smith, B.E.M. (*Jack Shaylor and the Lees*).

Berwick on Tweed* Northumberland 1835
Hon. Sec., Lieutenant-Commander G. Gibson; Coxswain, Henry Crombie (*William and Mary Durham*).

Bideford (*see* **Appledore**)

Blackpool* Lancashire 1864
Hon. Sec., Frederick L. Burton; Coxswain, Jim Stanhope (*Edgar, George, Orlando and Eva Child*).

Blackrock (Dundalk)	Co. Louth	1859	1935
Blakeney	Norfolk	Before 1825	1935
Blyth*	Northumberland	1826	

Hon. Sec., Dr Reginald Carr; Coxswain, Samuel Crawford (*Winston Churchill. Civil Service No. 8*).

Borth* Cardiganshire 1966
Hon. Sec., T. Aran-Morris

Boulmer	Northumberland	1825	1968
Bournemouth*	Hampshire	1965	1972 (I.L.B. 1972)

Hon. Sec., Commander Anthony D. Casswill, R.N.

Brancaster Norfolk 1874 1935

Braunton (*see* **Appledore**)

Bridgwater	Somerset	1836	Before 1850
Bridlington*	Yorkshire	1824	

Hon. Sec., Arthur W. Dick; Coxswain, John King (*William Henry and Mary King*).

Brighstone Grange	Isle of Wight	1860	1915
Brighton*	Sussex	1824	1931 (I.L.B. 1965)

Hon. Sec., H. C. Mileham

Brixham (*see* **Torbay**)

Station	*County*	*Date when station was established or taken over by the Institution*	*Date closed*
Broadstairs	Kent	1868	1912
Brooke	Isle of Wight	1860	1937
Broughty Ferry*	Angus	1830	
Hon. Sec., Captain R. W. Forbes and James T. Potter; Coxswain, Alick MacKay (*The Robert*).			
Buckhaven	Fife	1900	1932
Buckie	Banff	1860	
Hon. Sec., P. Kurray; Coxswain, Thomas Garden (*Laura Moncur*).			
Buddon Ness	Angus	1961	1894
Bude*	Cornwall	1837	1923 (I.L.B. 1966)
Hon. Sec., S. W. Whateley			
Bull Bay	Anglesey	1868	1926
Burnham	Somerset	1866	1930
Burnham-on-Crouch*	Essex	1966	
Hon. Sec., G. B. Law			
Burry Port	Carmarthenshire	1887	1914
Cadgwith	Cornwall	1867	
Cahore	Co. Wexford	1857	1916
Caister	Norfolk	1857	1969
Calshot	Hampshire	1972	
Hon. Sec., Colonel P. N. Keymer, M.C.; Coxswain, William Jones (*Ernest William and Elizabeth Ellen Hinde*).			
Camber (*see* **Rye**)			
Cambois (*see* **Blythe**)			
Campbeltown	Argyll	1861	
Hon. Sec., J. P. McWhirter; Coxswain, David Farmer (*City of Glasgow II*).			
Cardigan*	Cardiganshire	1849	1932 (I. L. B. 1970)
Hon. Sec., Captain J. B. James			
Carmarthen (*see* **Ferryside**)			
Carnsore	Co. Wexford	1859	1897
Carrickfergus	Co. Antrim	1896	1913
Castletown	Isle of Man	1856	1922
Cemaes	Anglesey	1872	1932
Cemlyn	Anglesey	1828	1919
Chapel	Lincolnshire	1870	1898
Chapman's Pool	Dorset	1866	1880
Chichester Harbour (*see* **Selsey**)			
Christchurch	Hampshire	1802	No record
Church Cove (*see* **Lizard**)			

Station	*County*	*Date when station was established or taken over by the Institution*	*Date closed*
Clacton-on-Sea*	Essex	1878	
Hon. Sec., Lieutenant-Commander C. J. White, R.N.V.R.; Coxswain, Charles Bolinbroke (*Valentine Wyndham-Quin*).			
Cleethorpes (*see* **Humber Mouth**)			
Clogher Head	Co. Louth	1899	
Hon. Sec., Mrs Marie C. Hoy; Coxswain, Michael Kirwan (*George and Caroline Ermen*).			
Cloughey-Portavogie	Co. Down	1885	
Hon. Sec., Captain M. Rutherford; Coxswain, John Donnan (*Glencoe, Glasgow*).			
Clovelly	Devonshire	1870	
Hon. Sec., Captain A. G. Sowman, C.B.E.; R.N.; Staff Coxswain, James Hunter (*Charley H. Barrett. Civil Service No. 35*).			
Conway*	Caernarvonshire	1966	
Hon. Sec., Richard H. Jones.			
Corton	Suffolk	1869	1879
Courtmacsherry	Co. Cork	1825	
Hon. Sec., J. O'Dwyer; Coxswain, John Barry (*Helen Wycherley*).			
Courtown	Co. Wexford	1865	1925
Coverack*	Cornwall	1901	1972 (I.L.B. 1972)
Hon. Sec., Lieutenant-Commander C. E. Sheen, D.S.C., R.N.; Coxswain, Vivian Carey (*William Taylor of Oldham*).			
Crail	Fife	1884	1923
Craster*	Northumberland	1969	
Hon. Sec., J. W. Robson			
Cresswell	Northumberland	1875	1944
Criccieth*	Caernarvonshire	1853	1968 (I.L.B. 1968)
Hon. Sec., Glyn Humphreys.			
Crimdon Dene*	Co. Durham	1966	
Hon. Sec., T. P. Reynolds.			
Cromarty	Ross & Cromarty	1911	1968
Cromer*	Norfolk	Before 1835	
Hon. Sec., Dr Paul S. Barclay, M.C., T.D.; Coxswain, Henry Davies, B.E.M. (*Ruby and Arthur Reed*).			
Cruden Bay (*see* **Port Erroll**)			
Culdaff	Co. Donegal	1872	1913
Cullercoats*	Northumberland	1852	1969 (I.L.B. 1969)
Hon. Sec., Alan Rankine.			

Station	*County*	*Date when station was established or taken over by the Institution*	*Date closed*
Dartmouth	Devonshire	1878	1896
Deal (*see* **North Deal**)			
Derrynane	Co. Kerry	1844	After 1850
Donaghadee	Co. Down	1910	
Hon. Sec., D. T. McKibbin; Coxswain, James Bunting (*Sir Samuel Kelly*).			
Donna Nook	Lincolnshire	1829	1931
Dornoch Firth and Embo	Sutherland	1886	1904
Douglas	Isle of Man	1802	
Hon. Sec., Captain T. H. Corteen; Coxswain, William Corran (*R. A. Colby Cubbin No 1.*).			
Dover	Kent	1837	
Hon. Sec., H. W. Andrews. Coxswain, Arthur Liddon (*Faithful Forester*).			
Drogheda	Co. Louth	1856	1926
Dublin (*see* **Poolbeg**)			
Dunbar*	East Lothian	1808	
Hon. Sec., William Gilmour; Coxswain, Robert Brunton (*Margaret*).			
Duncannon	Co. Wexford	1869	1886
Dundalk (*see* **Blackrock**)			
Dundee (*see* **Broughty Ferry**)			
Dundrum (*see* **Newcastle**)			
Dungarvan (*see* **Helvick Head**)			
Dungeness	Kent	1826	
Hon. Sec.; G. L. Bates; Coxswain, Tom Tart (*Mabel E. Holland*)			
Dun Laoghaire	Co. Dublin	Before 1825	
Hon. Sec., J. E. de Courcy Ireland; Coxswain, Eric Offer (*John F. Kennedy*)			
Dunmore East	Co. Waterford	1884	
Hon. Sec., J. S. Power; Coxswain, Stephen Whittle (*Dunleary II*).			
Dunwich	Suffolk	1873	1903
Easington	Yorkshire	1913	1933
Eastbourne*	Sussex	1822	
Hon. Sec., Alderman Cecil F. Baker, J.P.; Coxswain, Derek Huggett (*Beryl Tollemache*).			
Eastney*	Hampshire	1965	
Hon. Sec., Dr Ian T. McLachlan.			
Exmouth*	Devonshire	1803	
Hon. Sec., W. L. C. Smith; Coxswain, Brian Rowsell (*City of Birmingham*).			
Eyemouth	Berwick	1876	
Hon. Sec., Captain P. W. Gibson; Coxswain, Alexander Dougal (*Louise Stephens*).			

Station	*County*	*Date when station was established or taken over by the Institution*	*Date closed*
Falmouth	Cornwall	1867	
Hon. Sec., Captain F. H. Edwards; Coxswain, Walter West (*Lilla Maures, Douglas and Will*).			
Fenit	Co. Kerry	1879	1969
Ferryside	Carmarthenshire	1835	1960
Fethard	Co. Wexford	1886	1914
Filey*	Yorkshire	1823	
Hon. Sec., Philip Hodgson; Coxswain, Thomas Jenkinson (*Robert and Dorothy Hardcastle*).			
Fishguard	Pembrokeshire	1822	
Hon. Sec., N. O. Mabe; Coxswain, Glyn Bateman (*Howard Marryat*).			
Flamborough	Yorkshire	1871	
Hon. Sec., T. Woodhouse, O.B.E., J.P.; Coxswain, George Pockley (*Friendly Forester*).			
Fleetwood*	Lancashire	1859	
Hon. Sec., Richard T. Willoughby, T.D.; Coxswain, Roy Mitchinson (*Ann Letitia Russell*).			
Flint*	Flintshire	1966	
Hon. Sec., K. R. G. Parkington.			
Folkestone	Kent	1893	1930
Formby	Lancashire	1894	1919
Fowey	Cornwall	1859	
Hon. Sec., Captain J. G. Wilson, D.S.C., R.D., R.N.R.; Coxswain, James Turpin (*Deneys Reitz*).			
Fraserburgh	Aberdeen	1831	1973
Hon. Sec., Captain J. Carter.			
Galway Bay	Co. Galway	1927	
Hon. Sec., The Very Rev. Father O'Morain; Coxswain, Coleman Hernon (*Joseph Hiram Chadwick*).			
Giles Quay	Co. Louth	1879	1912
Girvan	Ayr	1865	
Hon. Sec., Captain J. W. Brown; Coxswain, William Coull (*James and Barbara Aitken*).			
Gourdon	Kincardine	1878	1969
Gt. Yarmouth and Gorleston*	Norfolk	Before 1825	
Hon. Sec., J. S. Ling; Coxswain, John Bryan (*Khami*)			
Greencastle	Co. Donegal	1864	1928
Greenore	Co. Louth	1894	1920
Greystones	Co. Wicklow	1872	1896
Grimsby	Lincolnshire	1868	1927

Station	*County*	*Date when station was established or taken over by the Institution*	*Date closed*
Groomsport	Co. Down	1858	1920
Guernsey (see **St Peter Port**)			
Happisburgh*	Norfolk	1965	
Hon. Sec., B. E. Trett.			
Hartlepool*	Co. Durham	Before 1825	
Hon. Sec., P. A. I. Farquhar.			
Harwich*	Essex	Before 1836	
Hon. Sec., Captain J. D. Gibson; Coxswain, Peter Burwood (*Margaret Graham*).			
Haisborough	Norfolk	1866	1926
Hastings*	Sussex	1858	
Hon. Sec., J. J. Adams; Coxswain, John Martin (*Fairlight*).			
Hauxley	Northumberland	1852	1939
Hayle	Cornwall	1866	1920
Hayling Island	Hampshire	1865	1924
Helensburgh*	Dunbarton	1965	
Hon. Sec., Alfred E. Thurgood.			
Helvick Head	Co. Waterford	1859	1969
Hendon Beach (*see* **Sunderland**)			
Hilbre Island	Cheshire	1848	1939
Holyhead*	Anglesey	1828	
Hon. Sec., Tudor B. Roberts; Coxswain, William Jones (*St Cybi, Civil Service No. 9*).			
Holy Island	Northumberland	1802	1968
Hope Cove	Devonshire	1878	1930
Hornsea	Yorkshire	1854	1924
Horton and Port Eynon*	Glamorgan	1968	
Hon. Sec., D. H. Farmer.			
Hove (*see* **Brighton**)			
Howth*	Co. Dublin	Before 1825	
Hon. Sec., J. Norman Wilkinson, D.S.C.; Coxswain, Gerald McLoughlin (*A.M.T.*).			
Hoylake	Cheshire	1803	
Hon. Sec., W. E. Kirkbride; Coxswain, Harold Triggs (*Thomas Corbett*).			
Humber	Yorkshire	1810	
Superintendent Coxswain, Robertson Buchan (*City of Bradford III*).			
Humber Mouth* (Cleethorpes)	Lincolnshire	1965	
Hon. Sec., Stanley R. Meakings.			
Huna	Caithness	1877	1930
Hunstanton	Norfolk	Before 1825	1931
Hurst Castle	Hampshire	1824	No record

Station	*County*	*Date when station was established or taken over by the Institution*	*Date closed*
Hythe	Kent	1876	1940
Ilfracombe	Devonshire	1828	
Hon. Sec., Lieutenant-Commander C. D. Hines, D.S.M., R.N.; Coxswain, David Clemence (*Lloyd's II*).			
Irvine	Ayrshire	1834	1914
Islay	Inner Hebrides	1934	
Hon. Sec., Neil MacMillan; Coxswain, Donald McPhee (*Francis W. Wotherspoon of Paisley*).			
Isle of Arran (*see* **Kildonan**)			
Isle of Purbeck (*see* **Kimmeridge and Chapman's Pool**)			
Isle of Whithorn (*see* **Whithorn**)			
Jersey, St Catherine's*	Channel Islands	1969	
Hon. Sec., Captain R. S. Taylor.			
Jersey (*see* **St Helier**)			
Johnshaven	Kincardine	1890	1928
Kessingland	Suffolk	1867	1936
Kildonan	Isle of Arran, Bute	1870	1902
Killybegs	Co. Donegal	1941	1945
Killough	Co. Down	1901	1914
Kilmore	Co. Wexford	1847	
Hon. Sec., J. T. Sutton; Coxswain, James Bute (*Lady Murphy*).			
Kimmeridge	Dorset	1868	1896
Kinghorn*	Fife	1965	
Hon. Sec., Dr R. M. L. Weir.			
Kingsdown	Kent	1866	1927
Kingsgate	Kent	1862	1897
Kingstown (*see* **Dun Laoghaire**)			
Kinsale	Co. Cork	Before 1825	No record
Kippford*	Kirkcudbright	1966	
Hon. Sec., John McKay.			
Kirkcudbright	Kirkcudbright	1862	
Hon. Sec., Dr R. N. Rutherfurd; Coxswain, George Davidson, D.S.M., B.E.M. (*Mary Pullman*).			
Kirkwall	Orkney	1972	
Hon. Sec., Captain W. S. Sinclair; Staff Coxswain in command (*Grace Paterson Ritchie*).			
Largs*	Ayr	1964	
Hon. Sec., J. T. Watt			

Station	*County*	*Date when station was established or taken over by the Institution*	*Date closed*
Lerwick	Shetland	1930	
Hon. Sec., Magnus M. Shearer. Coxswain, George Leith (*Claude Cecil Staniforth*).			
Little and Broad Haven*	Pembrokeshire	1967	
Hon. Sec., Elson G. Phillips.			
Littlehampton	Sussex	1884	1921 (I.L.B. 1967)
Hon. Sec., Peter Cheney.			
Littlehaven	Pembrokeshire	1882	1921
Littlestone-on-Sea*	Kent	1966	
Hon. Sec., J. K. Boardman.			
Liverpool	Lancashire	Before 1802	No record
Lizard—Cadgwith	Cornwall	1859	
Hon. Sec., L. A. Britton; Coxswain, Maurice Legg (*The Duke of Cornwall. Civil Service No. 33*).			
Llanaelhaiarn	Caernarvonshire	1883	1901
Llanddwyn	Anglesey	1840	1907
Llandudno*	Caernarvonshire	1861	
Hon. Sec., Thomas Taylor; Coxswain, Meurig Davies (*Lily Wainwright*).			
Llandulas	Denbighshire	1869	1932
Llanelly (*see* **Pembury**)			
Lochinver	Sutherland	1967	
Hon. Sec., P. W. Hay; Coxswain, David McBain (*George Urie Scott*).			
Londonderry (*see* **Greencastle**)			
Longhope	Orkney	1874	
Hon. Sec., J. M. F. Groat; Coxswain, John Leslie (*The David and Elizabeth King and E.B.*).			
Looe	Cornwall	1866	1930
Lossiemouth	Moray	1859	1923
Lowestoft	Suffolk	1801	
Hon. Sec., M. W. Chapman; Coxswain, Thomas Knott (*Frederick Edward Crick*).			
Lydd (*see* **Dungeness**)			
Lyme Regis*	Dorset	1826	1932 (I.L.B. 1967)
Hon. Sec., Major-General R. W. Jelf, C.B.E.			
Lymington*	Hampshire	1965	
Hon. Sec., K. C. G. Bacon, M.M.			
Lynmouth	Devonshire	1869	1944
Lytham-St Anne's*	Lancashire	1851	
Hon. Sec., John Kennedy; Coxswain, Arthur Wignall (*Sarah Townsend Porritt*).			

Station	*County*	*Date when station was established or taken over by the Institution*	*Date closed*
Mablethorpe*	Lincolnshire	1851	
Hon. Sec., William D. Stoney.			
Machrihanish	Argyll	1911	1930
Mallaig	Inverness	1948	
Hon. Sec., A. A. McLellan; Coxswain, Charles Henderson (*E.M.M. Gordon Cubbin*).			
Margate*	Kent	1860	
Hon. Sec., Noel Richard Kingston; Coxswain, Alfred Manning (*North Foreland. Civil Service No. 11*).			
Maryport	Cumberland	1865	1949
Methil (*see* **Buckhaven**)			
Mevagissey	Cornwall	1869	1930
Middlesbrough	Yorkshire	1858	1895
Milford Haven (*see* **Angle**)			
Minehead*	Somerset	1901	
Hon. Sec., Commander E. R. Tyndale-Biscoe, R.N.; Coxswain, Stanley Rawle (*B.H.M.H.*).			
Moelfre*	Anglesey	1830	
Hon. Sec., Thomas Owens; Coxswain, William Roberts (*Watkins Williams*).			
Montrose	Angus	1800	
Hon. Sec., J. M. D. Smith; Coxswain, James Paton, B.E.M. (*Lady McRobert*).			
Moray Firth (*see* **Nairn**)			
Morecambe*	Lancashire	1966	
Hon. Sec., Sam Baxter.			
Morthoe *or* **Morte Bay**	Devonshire	1871	1900
Mostyn	Flintshire	1835	1851
Mudeford*	Hampshire	1965	
Hon. Sec., Ken Durham.			
Mullion	Cornwall	1867	1908
Mumbles*	Glamorgan	1866	
Hon. Sec., E. G. Beynon; Coxswain, Derek Scott, B.E.M. (*William Gammon—Manchester and District XXX*).			
Mundesley	Norfolk	Before 1825	1895
Nairn	Nairn	1878	1911
Newbiggin	Northumberland	1851	
Hon. Sec., A. D. Manley; Coxswain, Edward Dawson (*Mary Joicey*).			
New Brighton	Cheshire	1863	
Hon. Sec., Captain W. P. Duguid; Coxswain, William Morris (*Norman B. Corlett*).			
Newburgh	Aberdeen	1828	1965

Station	*County*	*Date when station was established or taken over by the Institution*	*Date closed*
Newcastle	Co. Down	1835	
Hon. Sec., Captain the Earl of Roden, R.N; Coxswain, Michael Leneghan (*William and Laura*).			
Newhaven	Sussex	1803	
Hon. Sec., R. K. Sayer, M.B.E.; Coxswain, Edgar Moore (*Kathleen Mary*).			
Newlyn	Cornwall	1908	1913
Newport	Pembrokeshire	1884	1894
Newquay*	Cornwall	1860	1945 (I.L.B. 1965)
Hon. Sec., Lewis J. C. Billingham.			
New Quay*	Cardiganshire	1864	
Hon. Sec., Captain Cosmo Jones; Coxswain, David Evans (*Birds Eye*).			
New Romney	Kent	1861	1928
Northam Burrows (*see* **Appledore**)			
North Berwick*	East Lothian	1860	1925 (I.L.B. 1967)
Hon. Sec., Lieutenant-Commander J. D. Tweedie, R.N.V.R.			
North Deal	Kent	1865	1932
North Deal Reserve	Kent	1915	1921
North Sunderland*	Northumberland	1827	
Hon. Sec., R. H. Reay; Coxswain, Robert Douglas (*The Edward and Mary Lester*).			
Oban*	Argyll	1972	
Hon. Sec., N. E. Budge.			
Ormes Head (*see* **Llandudno**)			
Padstow	Cornwall	Before 1825	
Hon. Sec., H. H. Lobb; Coxswain, Anthony Warnock (*James and Catherine Macfarlane*).			
Pakefield	Suffolk	1840	1922
Palling	Norfolk	1852	1930
Peel*	Isle of Man	1828	1972 (I.L.B. 1972)
Hon. Sec., Captain A. D. Watterson, I.L.B. (*Helena Harris—Manchester and District XXXI*).			
Pembery *or* **Pembury**	Carmarthenshire	1863	1887
Penarth	Glamorgan	1861	1905
Penlee and Penzance	Cornwall	1803	
Hon. Sec., D. L. Johnson; Coxswain, William Richards (*Solomon Browne*).			
Penmon	Anglesey	1832	1915

Station	*County*	*Date when station was established or taken over by the Institution*	*Date closed*
Penrhyndu	Merioneth	1844	1853
Peterhead	Aberdeen	1965	
Hon. Sec., W. A. P. Cormack; Coxswain, Alexander Birnie (*James and Mariska Joicey*).			
Piel (*see* **Barrow**)			
Pill*	Somerset	1971	
Hon. Sec., Pilot J. Rich, M.I.N., M.N.I.			
Plymouth*	Devonshire	1803	
Hon. Sec., Raymond H. E. Sainsbury; Coxswain, John Dare (*Thomas Forehead and Mary Rowse*).			
Point of Ayr	Flintshire	1894	1923
Polkerris (*see* **Fowey**)			
Poolbeg	Co. Dublin	1820	1959
Poole*	Dorset	1865	
Hon. Sec., Major John Showell-Rogers, R.M.; Coxswain, Reginald Brown (*George Elmy*).			
Port Askaig (*see* **Islay**)			
Port Ellen (*see* **Islay**)			
Port Erin	Isle of Man	1883	
Hon. Sec., R. Rimington; Coxswain, Peter Woodworth (*Matthew Simpson*).			
Port Erroll	Aberdeen	1877	1921
Port Eynon (*see* **Horton**)	Glamorgan	1884	1916
Porthcawl*	Glamorgan	1860	1902 (I.L.B. 1965)
Hon. Sec., John Blundell.			
Porthdinllaen	Caernarvonshire	1864	
Hon. Sec., J. E. Roberts, M.B.E., J.P.; Coxswain, Thomas Moore (*Charles Henry Ashley*).			
Porthleven	Cornwall	1863	1929
Porthoustock	Cornwall	1869	1942
Porth Rhuffydd	Anglesey	1891	1904
Port Isaac*	Cornwall	1869	1933
Hon. Sec., Raymond M. Harris.			
Portloe *or* **Portlor**	Cornwall	1870	1887
Portland	Dorset	1826	1850
Port Logan	Wigtown	1866	1932
Portmadoc (*see* **Criccieth**)			
Portpatrick	Wigtown	1877	
Hon. Sec., J. Campbell; Coxswain, Andrew Mitchell (*The Jeanie*).			

Station	*County*	*Date when station was established or taken over by the Institution*	*Date closed*
Portrush	Co. Antrim	1860	
Hon. Sec., W. R. Knox, C.B.E., M.M., J.P.; Coxswain, Robert McMullan (*Lady Scott. Civil Service No. 4*).			
Port St Mary*	Isle of Man	1896	
Hon. Sec., J. Hudson; Coxswain, John Gawne, B.E.M. (*R.A. Colby Cubbin No. 2*).			
Port Talbot (Aberavon Beach)*	Glamorgan	1966	
Hon. Sec., David F. Aubrey.			
Purbeck Island (*see* **Chapman's Pool**)			
Pwllheli*	Caernarvonshire	1891	
Hon. Sec., Captain D. C. Evans; Coxswain, William McGill (*Anthony Robert Marshall*).			
Queensferry*	West Lothian	1967	
Hon. Sec., Captain J. F. Kersley.			
Queenstown	Co. Cork	1866	1920
Ramsey	Isle of Man	1829	
Hon. Sec., B. T. Swales; Coxswain, Lawrence Gawne (*James Bell Ritchie*).			
Ramsgate*	Kent	1802	
Hon. Sec., K. F. Speakman; Coxswain, Thomas Cooper (*Michael and Lily Davis*).			
Red Bay*	Co. Antrim	1972	
Hon. Sec., Captain T. L. Scollay.			
Redcar*	Yorkshire	1802	
Hon. Sec., Frank Cockcroft; Coxswain, Ronald Dixon (*Sir James Knott*).			
Rhoscolyn	Anglesey	1830	1929
Rhosneigr	Anglesey	1872	1924
Rhyl*	Flintshire	1852	
Hon. Sec., John M. Owen; Coxswain, William Hunt (*Har-Lil*).			
Robin Hood's Bay	Yorkshire	1830	1931
Roe Island (*see* **Peel**)			
Rogerstown	Co. Dublin	1874	1882
Roker (*see* **Sunderland**)			
Rosslare Harbour	Co. Wexford	1838	
Hon. Sec., C. G. Miller; Coxswain, Richard Walsh (*R. Hope Roberts*).			
Rosslinks (*see* **Holy Island**)			
Rossglass	Co. Dublin	1825	1835
Runswick	Yorkshire	1866	
Hon. Sec., H. Roddom; Coxswain, Colin Harrison (*The Royal Thames*).			

Station	*County*	*Date when station was established or taken over by the Institution*	*Date closed*
Ryde	Isle of Wight	1869	1923
Rye	Sussex	1803	1901
Rye Harbour*	Sussex	1803	1928 (I.L.B. 1966)
Hon. Sec., Humphrey Lestocq.			
St Abbs	Berwick	1911	
Hon. Sec., E. Greene; Coxswain, James Wilson, B.E.M. (*Jane Hay*).			
St Agnes*	Cornwall	1968	
Hon. Sec., C. J. Whitworth.			
St Agnes	Scilly Isles	1890	1920
St Andrews	Fife	1800	1938
St Anne's (*see also* **Lytham-St Anne's**)	Lancashire	1881	1925
St Bees*	Cumberland	1930	
Hon. Sec., Captain James Gibbons, D.S.C.			
St Brides (*see* **Littlehaven**)			
St David's	Pembrokeshire	1869	
Hon. Sec., W. Llewellyn; Coxswain, William Morris (*Joseph Soar, Civil Service No. 34*).			
St Helier	Jersey	1884	
Hon. Sec., Captain R. S. Taylor; Coxswain, Michael Berry (*Elizabeth Rippon*).			
St Ives*	Cornwall	1840	
Hon. Sec., Captain E. Kemp; Coxswain, Thomas Cocking (*Frank Penfold Marshall*).			
St Mary's	Scilly Isles	1837	
Hon. Sec., Captain A. J. Jenkins; Coxswain, Matthew Lethbridge (*Guy and Clare Hunter*).			
St Peter Port	Guernsey	1803	
Hon. Sec., Captain J. C. Allez; Coxswain, John Petit (*Arun*).			
St Sampsons (*see* **St Peter Port**)			
Salcombe	Devonshire	1869	
Hon. Sec., W. P. Budgett; Coxswain, John Griffiths (*The Baltic Exchange*).			
Saltburn	Yorkshire	1849	1922
Scarborough*	Yorkshire	1801	
Hon. Sec., Major R. F. Soper, M.B.E.; Coxswain, William Sheader (*J. G. Graves of Sheffield*). (Inflatable: *Young People of Scarborough*)			
Scilly Isles (*see* **St Mary's**)			
Seaham	Co. Durham	1970	
Hon. Sec., Leslie Hood; Coxswain, Arthur Farrington (*The Will and Fanny Kirby*).			
Seascale	Cumberland	1875	1895
Seaton Carew	Co. Durham	Before 1835	1922

Station	*County*	*Date when station was established or taken over by the Institution*	*Date closed*
Seaton Snook	Co. Durham	1907	1909
Selsey*	Sussex	1861	
Hon. Sec., Desmond Cockayne; Coxswain, William Jones (*Charles Henry*).			
Sennen Cove	Cornwall	1853	
(Temporarily non-operational)			
Sheerness*	Kent	1972	
Hon. Sec., Captain D. Gibbons. Coxswain, Charles Bowry (*Gertrude*).			
Sheringham	Norfolk	1839	
Hon. Sec., J. R. Bell; Coxswain, Robert West (*The Manchester Unity of Odd Fellows*).			
Shoreham Harbour*	Sussex	1865	
Hon. Sec., John C. Harrison; Coxswain, John Fox (*Dorothy and Philip Constant*).			
Sidmouth	Devonshire	1869	1912
Silloth*	Cumberland	1860	(1896 I.L.B. 1967)
Hon. Sec., Michael Saul.			
Skateraw	East Lothian	1907	1943
Skegness*	Lincolnshire	1825	
Hon. Sec., F. N. Ball; Coxswain, Kenneth Holland (*Charles Fred Grantham*).			
Skerries	Co. Dublin	1854	1930
Solva	Pembrokeshire	1869	1887
Southend Cantyre	Argyll	1869	1930
Southend-on-Sea*	Essex	1879	
Hon. Sec., P. G. Garon, M.C., G.M.; Coxswain, Peter Gilson (*Greater London II, Civil Service No. 30*).			
Southport	Lancashire	1860	1925
Southsea	Hampshire	1886	1918
Southwold*	Suffolk	1852	1940 (I.L.B. 1963)
Hon. Sec., John Adnams.			
Spurn (*see* **Humber**)			
Staithes	Yorkshire	1875	1938
Stonehaven*	Kincardine	1867	1934 (I.L.B. 1967)
Hon. Sec., James Elliot.			
Stornoway	Isle of Lewis, Hebrides	1887	
Hon. Sec., Captain Alexander Mackay; Coxswain, Roderick Maclean (*The James and Margaret Boyd*).			
Stromness	Orkney	1867	
Hon. Sec., Captain J. Allan; Coxswain, Alfred Sinclair (*Archibald and Alexander M. Paterson*).			

Station	*County*	*Date when station was established or taken over by the Institution*	*Date closed*
Stronsay	Orkney	1909	1972
Hon. Sec., Andrew Burghes; Coxswain, James Stout (*The John Gellatly Hyndman*).			
Studland	Dorset	1826	1852
Sunderland*	Co. Durham	1800	
Hon. Sec., Captain William W. White; Coxswain, John Todd (*William Myers and Sarah Jane Myers*).			
Sutton	Lincolnshire	1844	1913
Swanage	Dorset	1875	
Hon. Sec., Captain D. A. N. Aldridge; Coxswain, Ronald Hardy (*R.L.P.*).			
Swansea (*see* **Mumbles**)			
Teesmouth	Yorkshire	1911	
Hon Sec., E. R. Copeman; Coxswain, William Carter (*Sarah Jane and James Season*).			
Teignmouth	Devonshire	Before 1825	1940
Tenby*	Pembrokeshire	1852	
Hon. Sec., G. Reason-Jones; Coxswain, Joshua Richards (*Henry Comber Brown*).			
Theddlethorpe	Lincolnshire	1864	1882
Thorpeness *or* **Thorpe**	Suffolk	1853	1900
Thurso	Caithness	1860	
Hon. Sec., Captain A. A. Munro; Coxswain, Gilbert Reid (*The Three Sisters*).			
Tighnabruiach	Argyll	1967	
Hon. Sec., Dr George L. Thomson.			
Tobermory	Hebrides	1938	1947
Torbay*	Devonshire	1866	
Hon. Sec., Alderman Frederick W. H. Park, M.B.E.; Coxswain, Kenneth Gibbs (*Princess Alexandra of Kent*).			
Torquay	Devonshire	1876	1923
Totland Bay	Isle of Wight	1885	1924
Tralee Bay (*see* **Fenit**)			
Tramore*	Co. Waterford	1858	1924 (I.L.B. 1964)
Hon. Sec., Finian P. Mongey.			
Tre-Arddur Bay*	Anglesey	1967	
Hon. Sec., Tudor B. Roberts.			
Troon	Ayr	1871	
Hon. Sec., T. M. Brown; Coxswain, Edward Brooks (*Connel Elizabeth Cargill*).			
Tynemouth*	Northumberland	1862	
Hon. Sec., Kenneth Middlemiss; Coxswain, Robert Burnton (*Tynesider*)			
Tyrella	Co. Down	1860	1899

Station	*County*	*Date when station was established or taken over by the Institution*	*Date closed*
Upgang	Yorkshire	1865	1919

Valentia Co. Kerry 1864
Hon. Sec. P. J. Gallagher; Coxswain Dermot Walsh (*Rowland Watts*).

Walmer* Kent 1856
Hon. Sec., Alderman Cavell; Coxswain, Henry Brown (*Charles Dibdin, Civil Service No. 32*).

Walton and Frinton Essex 1884
Hon. Sec., R. Oxley, J.P.; Coxswain, Frank Bloom (*Edian Courtauld*).

Watchet Somerset 1875 1944

Wells* Norfolk 1869
Hon. Sec., Lieutenant David J. Case, R.N.V.R.; Coxswain, David Cox (*Ernest Tom Neathercoat*).

West Hartlepool Co. Durham 1869 1906

West Kirby* Cheshire 1966
Hon. Sec., W. E. Kirkbride.

West Mersea* Essex 1963
Hon. Sec., Lieutenant-Commander Maurice W. Bond, R.N.R.

Weston-super-Mare* Somerset 1882
Hon. Sec., Clifford Smith.

Westport Co. Mayo 1857 1860

West Wittering (*see* **Selsey**)

Wexford (*see* **Rosslare**)

Weymouth Dorset 1869
Hon. Sec., Kenneth H. Mooring Aldridge; Coxswain, Alfred Pavey (*Frank Spiller Locke*).

Whitburn Co. Durham 1830 1918

Whitby* Yorkshire 1802
Hon. Sec., Eric Thomson; Coxswain, William Harland (*Mary Ann Hepworth*).

Whitehaven Cumberland 1804 1925

Whitehills Banff 1860 1969

Whitelink Bay Aberdeen 1878 1905

Whithorn, Isle of Wigtown 1869 1919

Whitstable* Kent 1963
Hon. Sec., B. E. Hardy, M.I.C.E.

Station	*County*	*Date when station was established or taken over by the Institution*	*Date closed*
Wick	Caithness	1895	
Hon. Sec., Captain M. D. MacKenzie; Coxswain, Donald McKay (*Princess Marina*).			
Wicklow	Co. Wicklow	1857	
Hon. Sec., James L. Kavanagh; Coxswain, Charles Byrne (*J. W. Archer*).			
Winchelsea (*see* **Rye Harbour**)			
Winterton	Norfolk	1857	1924
Withernsea	Yorkshire	1862	1913
Woodbridge Haven	Suffolk	1801	1852
Workington	Cumberland	1886	
Hon. Sec., R. Atkinson; Coxswain, Albert Brown (*Manchester and Salford XXIX*).			
Worthing	Sussex	1852	1930
Yarmouth (*see* **Gorleston**)			
Yarmouth*	Isle of Wight	1924	
Hon. Sec., L. W. Noton; Coxswain, David Kenneth (*The Earl and Countess Howe*).			
Yealm River	Devonshire	1878	1927
Youghal	Co. Cork	1839	
Hon. Sec., Commander B. K. C. Arbuthnot, D.S.C., R.N.; Coxswain, Christopher Hennessy (*Grace Darling*).			

Appendix IV

TYPES OF OFFSHORE LIFE-BOAT NOW IN SERVICE

Clyde 70 ft. steel
Arun 52 ft.
Barnett 52 ft.
Thames 50 ft. steel
Solent 48 ft. 6 in. steel
Oakley 48 ft. 6 in.; 37 ft.
Beach 42 ft.; 41 ft.
Waveney 44 ft. steel
Keith Nelson 40 ft. glass reinforced plastic
Rother 37 ft.
Liverpool 35 ft. 6 in.

TYPES OF INSHORE LIFE-BOAT

INFLATABLE
also 21 ft.
19 ft.
18 ft.
17 ft.

Appendix V

PRINCIPAL AWARDS OF THE INSTITUTION

For operational service:

Gold Medal: Instituted 1824
The Institution's highest award for gallantry in sea-rescue. Very occasionally given as a mark of distinction to corporate bodies or individuals. Total of gold medals and clasps awarded, to 1973, 132.

Silver Medal: Instituted 1824
Total of silver medals and clasps awarded, to 1973, 1,499.

Bronze Medal: Instituted 1917
Total of bronze medals and clasps awarded, to 1973, 562.

Thanks Inscribed on Vellum:

Medal Service Certificates: Instituted 1955
Awarded to crew members in rescues which have justified the giving of medals to individuals in the boat or boats concerned.

Note. Holders of the Institution's medals, if wearing the uniform of the Armed Services, wear the blue ribbon on the right breast, as in the case of certain other life-saving awards. (One of Sir William Hillary's medals, now belonging to the Institution, has, by way of contrast, a red ribbon.) The dolphin clasp attaching the medal to the ribbon is noteworthy. When the ribbon alone is worn, holders of the gold medal show on it a miniature of Hillary's head: this miniature also signifies the award of second service clasps or bars for acts of gallantry following the first for which a medal was given.

For services to the Institution:

Honorary Life Governorship: Instituted 1921

Gold Badge: Instituted 1912
Awarded in recognition of at least twenty years' exceptionally good service. A bar (instituted 1956) may be awarded after further service, normally of not less than five years.

Silver Badge: Instituted 1956
Normally given to Honorary Secretaries after ten years' service as such, and for equivalent work.

Gold and Silver Brooches:
Awarded to women for exceptional services to the Institution, with bars as appropriate.

Framed Records of Thanks: Instituted 1918

Framed Letters of Thanks signed by the Chairman of the Committee of Management: Instituted 1966

Appendix VI

ANNUAL RECEIPTS

1824..£9,706	1867..£39,305	1902..£105,454	1938..£349,882
1825..£9,826	1868..£31,668	1903..£112,704	1939..£284,153
1826..£3,392	1869..£14,409	1904..£118,507	1940..£356,321
1827..£1,269	1870..£25,711	1905..£114,007	1941..£386,836
1828..£1,234	1871..£28,140	1906..£121,073	1942..£495,775
1829..£1,324	1872..£27,331	1907..£103,793	1943..£528,726
1830..£2,425	1873..£31,740	1908..£115,303	1944..£563,507
1831..£835	1874..£33,500	1909..£126,215	1945..£609,294
1832..£984	1875..£39,835	1910..£97,322	1946..£588,541
1833..£1,615	1876..£33,801	1911..£113,352	1947..£619,944
1834..£2,227	1877..£42,442	1912..£110,908	1948..£689,125
1835..£806	1878..£34,493	1913..£122,966	1949..£577,638
1836..£788	1879..£30,125	1914..£111,813	1950..£741,863
1837..£899	1880..£38,507	1915..£139,606	1951..£655,861
1838..£554	1881..£36,419	1916..£146,948	1952..£739,708
1839..£743	1882..£43,117	1917..£150,844	1953..£775,040
1840..£1,582	1883..£40,250	1918..£181,003	1954..£864,235
1841..£729	1884..£44,810	1919..£151,025	1955..£837,675
1842/9..not recorded.		1920..£185,903	1956..£1,001,209
1850..£354	1885..£47,035	1921..£174,501	1957..£997,848
1851..£758	1886..£43,044	1922..£91,399	1958..£1,118,684
1852..£2,468	1887..£56,970	1923..£180,014	1959..£973,322
1853..£703	1888..£50,813	1924..£241,780	1960..£1,023,629
1854..£1,885	1889..£42,700	1925..£235,818	1961..£1,234,909
1855..£1,744	1890..£42,523	1926..£211,964	1962..£1,355,792
1856..£4,983	1891..£65,295	1927..£228,975	1963..£1,530,541
1857..£5,327	1892..£58,527	1928..£299,263	1964..£1,695,282
1858..£6,112	1893..£56,550	1929..£311,054	1965..£1,598,334
1859..£10,633	1894..£73,526	1930..£319,434	1966..£1,721,485
1860..£14,027	1895..£81,159	1931..£264,040	1967..£1,521,124
1861..£15,092	1896..£117,036	1932..£268,588	1968..£1,819,887
1862..£14,825	1897..£81,569	1933..£294,916	1969..£2,173,508
1863..£21,101	1898..£108,625	1934..£309,584	1970..£2,419,259
1864..£31,917	1899..£105,176	1935..£321,861	1971..£2,501,380
1865..£28,932	1900..£101,184	1936..£293,915	1972..£3,123,277
1866..£41,718	1901..£107,293	1937..£308,015	

Appendix VII

R.N.L.I. HOUSE FLAG AND ENSIGN

The original flag of the Institution was made in about 1884 by Miss Leonora Frances Margaret Preston, sister of one of the Committee of Management. It is made up of the Red Cross of St George, edged with blue on a white field. The letters R.N.L.I. are placed one in the centre of each canton. In the centre of the flag is a yellow crown, above a yellow anchor.

In December 1964 the Ministry of Defence issued a Warrant authorizing the Institution's boats to fly a Red Ensign defaced by its house flag.

The life-boat fleet is registered in London. When stationed in the Irish Republic, life-boats fly the Irish Tricolor.